GOD MADE KNOWN

❖ ❖ ❖ ❖ ❖ ❖ ❖ ❖

GOD MADE KNOWN

❖ ❖ ❖ ❖ ❖

Thomas A. Langford

CHARLES W. BROCKWELL, JR.
GENERAL EDITOR

ABINGDON PRESS / Nashville

GOD MADE KNOWN

Copyright © 1992 by Abingdon Press

This book is printed on recycled, acid-free paper.

Library of Congress Cataloging-in-Publication Data

LANGFORD, THOMAS A.
    God made known / Thomas A. Langford.
        p.   cm—(We believe)
    Includes bibliographical references.
    ISBN 0-687-17976-9 (alk. paper)
        1. United Methodist Church (U.S.)—Doctrines. 2. Methodist
    Church—Doctrines. I. Series.
    BX8382.2.Z5L36   1992
    230'.76—dc20   92-332
                                                                      CIP

MANUFACTURED IN THE UNITED STATES OF AMERICA

To the members of the
Western North Carolina
Annual Conference

CONTENTS

Contents

FOREWORD

*J*ohn Wesley has been described as a "folk theologian." His own stated purpose in communication was to speak "plain truth for plain people." He did this in his widely circulated tracts. In his preaching, he spoke the common language and was able to reach the hearts of the multitudes.

In this book, Thomas Langford follows in the tradition of encouraging the "common folk" to be responsible theologians. The purpose of the book is to lead the reader to undertake theological reflection. The book is written so uncertain laypersons may understand and begin the process of "doing theology."

This is a timely book. United Methodists have not always known what to do with theology. They have rejected doctrinaire rigidity. They have been proud of their acceptance of a broad spectrum of beliefs. The result is that many have done little or no theological reflection.

Since our new theological statement was adopted in 1988, there has been widespread study of this document. Bishops, district superintendents, pastors, and laypersons have all been involved. But something has been lacking.

Many laypersons I know have been looking for a resource to do what this book does. They believe that the whole church is to "do theology." This book will help the average person get a handle on this task.

The book does not make excessive claims. It does not promise to provide answers. Dr. Langford recognizes that, even with the most profound reflection, God is still a mystery. The book does open the path to reflection on God and life. I believe it will lead people in the local church to deeper understanding of the gospel and will be a source of inspiration for those who take it seriously.

This book is another contribution of Dr. Langford to the entire church. The people who have been called "to reform the nation" and "spread scriptural holiness over the land" have been unclear about their mission in recent years. The use of this book may help laypersons hear the energizing call of God again.

Persons who use this book in groups with others will feel the power of God anew and will become witnesses to God's work among us.

R. Sheldon Duecker

PREFACE

Bishop R. Sheldon Duecker has asserted, "United Methodists don't have a *common* understanding of basic Christian beliefs." He has reported a layperson saying to him, "I hunger for a clear sense of my United Methodist *identity*."

What is United Methodist doctrine? Many voices respond to this question, ranging from those hoping to instruct the Church to caucuses intending to pressure it.

None of these voices, however, speaks for the Church. "No person, no paper, no organization, has the authority to speak officially for The United Methodist Church, this right having been reserved officially for The United Methodist Church, this right having been reserved exclusively to the General Conference under the Constitution" (*The Discipline*, par. 610.1).

This book is the second of a series called "We Believe." This is a series of books written for United Methodist laypersons to advance self-understanding and identity by communicating United Methodist doctrine directly from General Conference approved documents.

The authors have set forth what the Church officially teaches rather than what each thinks the Church ought to teach. They focus on the question: "What theological teaching has The United Methodist Church 'owned' through its established conciliar processes of decision making and teaching?"

Thus these books are not personal statements or caucus declarations. They present the teachings of John Wesley; *The Book of Discipline;* and other official United Methodist documents (e.g., *The Book of Resolutions; The United Methodist Hymnal, The Book of Services*).

The authors in this series do not proceed by linking up the categories of systematic theology and saying what the Church teaches under each heading. They pursue core elements of "substantial, experimental, practical divinity" through the Church's own documents. This method of beginning with how doctrine affects Christian life is characteristically Wesleyan.

John Wesley used our doctrines to specify the scriptural, historic Christian teachings that were the particular emphases of "the work of God called Methodism." Primarily, these were teachings relating to divine-human interaction and to sanctification. The books in this series remind us of this heritage and include United Methodist, not just Wesleyan, doctrine.

What might these books do for The United Methodist Church? (1) They will bring before the Church its common body of official doctrinal sources and survey what these sources teach. (2) They will demonstrate how the Church's workbooks and worship books are doctrinal documents.

(3) This will advance the teaching office of the General Conference. (4) They will point out where the Church's doctrine needs clarification and better organization for consistency and coherence. (5) They will promote discussion of whether the Church needs a theological secretariat to assist our highest governing council in defining United Methodist doctrine.

The United Methodist Church is part of the community of Wesleyan denominations, but The United Methodist Church has larger responsibilities. One of these is the formal development of doctrine. The books in this series contribute to the maturing of that ministry among and for "the people called United Methodists."

Charles W. Brockwell, Jr.
General Editor

INTRODUCTION

*U*nited Methodism possesses a theology. That is, our Church has developed understandings of God that provide a foundation for Christian living and clarity of meaning for Christian witness. Our effort in this book is to explore the roots and flowering of our beliefs. We shall look at the way The United Methodist Church undertakes the task of understanding and interpreting God.

Is a study of how United Methodists think about their Christian faith too narrow? Does such an effort imply denominational self-centeredness, even pettiness? Does concentration on a particular church deny ecumenical sensitivity? To all of these questions we answer with a strong *no.*

Everyone lives within specific traditions, whether cultural, social, or religious. Traditions provide us with backgrounds and horizons. From our traditions we receive our language and our sense of what is important. Our traditions provide us with heroes and heroines, with a sense of what is good and valuable, and with a sense of past, present, and future. Consequently, we need a clear recognition of the traditions by which we are shaped.

Our tradition is where we are forced to begin. But past tradition is not where we shall end. United Methodists have been shaped by a particular church tradition, and this tradition has made us forward-looking. To grow up in Methodism is to be aware of our indebtedness to other traditions and to anticipate worship and service with other Christians. Good upbringing in this tradition makes us ready for new growth that reaches beyond our inheritance. Deep roots produce new fruit.

The study of United Methodist theology must recognize the actual church context in which we have been reared: A context of which we can make positive use, and—equally important—a context with which we must struggle. To be shaped by a tradition means not only to receive its gifts with appreciation, but also to recognize the people and the ideas with which we must contend. A vital tradition may be characterized as an extended debate; it is with one's parents that many of the sharpest expressions of love and struggle occur.

This book represents a study of United Methodist theology as it is expressed in official statements by our church. We shall draw attention to and explain the meaning of our formally presented theological understandings, especially those found in our *Book of Discipline* (this is made clear in chapter 3). We shall discuss how United Methodists think about their faith.

The study of United Methodist theology should keep us aware of our past and our present, our Christian community and our world setting, and our faith and our service. The promise of United Methodist theological work is found in building on our tradition in order "to serve the present age."

CHAPTER I

Beginning

Theology is an off-putting word. So why is it important and why should ordinary believers care about such a thing?

The issue is rather simple: Theology is thinking about God; everyone who thinks about God is practicing theology. When Christians talk about God they are talking theologically. Hence, whether we want to be or not, we are theologians because we do talk about God.

This description, of course, may be an exaggeration. Not everyone who is interested in stars or who talks about stars is an astronomer—not in a technical sense. But when we begin to care about the stars and attempt to understand them, we turn to professional astronomers to enlighten us. We learn from physicists and, then, our knowledge reflects these professional descriptions of the heavens. Therefore, in limited ways we are astronomers.

But we may also talk about the stars as poets. We may express awe or wonder. Words may be put to music; emotions may be put to action. Thus we can talk about the stars in a variety of ways—as astronomers or as poets—depending on our perspective. No single viewpoint is complete in itself, neither the poet nor the astronomer captures the full meaning of the stars. Stars may also be used. Navigators reckon their course by stars; physicists measure the age of the universe by the life of stars; we calculate seasons of the year by stars. It was an immense intellectual achievement of ancient people to observe—with remarkable accuracy—over extended time and describe the arrangement and changing location of stars.

On the other hand, distortions of the meaning of stars can occur. Astrologers see in stars the fatal control of human lives. Our destinies, they claim, are written in the stars. Such interpreters, such stargazers, may be dangerous because misuses can misinterpret and misguide life.

As we attempt to observe and talk about stars, we are debtors to all those who have studied, described, and calculated on the basis of stars. We learn from some and deny the views of others. As we become serious astronomers, we become—even if in limited ways—physicists and poets, romantics and singers, critics and judges, for our understanding of the stars is filtered through all of these perspectives, and the history each carries with it.

So also with our interest in God. As the love of God commands our lives, we attempt to understand who God is. We listen to those who are acknowledged as authorities: Scripture, our foreparents in faith, our own experience, and our ability to reason and judge.

Some people in the church are by profession theologians—we might call them religion's astronomers. These are persons educated to know

Scripture and tradition, to study experience, and to express ideas with logical rigor. These people help lead the Church in its theological reflection.

But the work of professional theologians is not a substitute for careful consideration of theological issues by every thoughtful Christian. Theologians, strictly speaking, do not act as spokespersons for the Church; they lead and guide the Church as a community in thoughtful reflection on God. The 1988 United Methodist theological statement puts it this way, "Scholars have their role to play in assisting the people of God to fulfill this calling [to be theologically engaged], but all Christians are called to theological reflection."[1] (This quotation is from *The Book of Discipline of the United Methodist Church.* Throughout our discussion this will be our primary point of reference. Look at notes 1, 4, and 8 at the back of this book for more explicit comments about this source.)

As Christians, we listen to theologians, people such as St. Augustine and Thomas Aquinas, Martin Luther and John Calvin, John Wesley and contemporary persons who seek to understand God. We also listen to poets and we sing hymns; we watch the lives of exemplary Christians; we attempt to serve our neighbors; we worship and pray, we share our thoughts, our sorrows, our joys, and our hopes with others. We are theologians, as we are shaped by all of these experiences and as we think and talk about God.

WHOLENESS OF THOUGHT AND LIFE

To say we are theologians is not an act of pride, it is simply a recognition of place and responsibility.

As a teenager I worked in a grocery store. In my first weeks there I found myself answering questions like, "Where is the soap?" with the impersonal reply, "They have that on the third aisle," as if I was not a part of the store. Later, without being aware of the transition, I found myself saying, "We have that on the third aisle." I was part of the place; I accepted responsibility. I was a grocer.

To grow in faith, to teach a church school class, to visit and talk with a sick friend, to share a tragedy, to sing a song, to say, "Life is good," or "Life is a vale of tears": To do any of these things, a person of faith engages life as a theologian. To be a theologian means to be a part of a Christian community; it is to begin to think about, talk about, sing about, and act on one's faith. In a basic sense, everyone who worships God and thinks about God is a theologian. The real question is: How responsible are we as theologians?

A person does not have to be a theologian in any strict sense in order to be a Christian. Some people love deeply, act truly, and live with God without devoting much thought to what they do. And often they are more committed Christians than those who talk too glibly, attempt to conquer immense intellectual worlds, or are always attempting to argue about religious issues. Nonetheless, insofar as one does think about her or his faith, that person is a theologian, and that person should accept responsibility for careful, devoted thought and speech.

To be a Christian is to attempt to live a whole life; that is, to be a Christian is to try to keep together one's thoughts, one's feelings, and one's actions. Yet, it is not unusual to find people who attempt to live with their thoughts separated from their emotions, and their actions unrelated to their deepest beliefs. But to do so is to live in a broken, splintered, partial way. Holding all of the dimensions of life together is no easy task, but to move toward cohesion and integration is a sign of Christian maturity.

Theology is only a part of our total personal statement. Theology tends to emphasize the rational dimension of life and this is important, for we are to love God with our minds. But rationality is only one aspect of our total being, for we are to love God also with our hearts and our strength. Christian maturity means to be drawn toward a complete love of God: to obey the great commandment (Matt. 22:37-39).

Christian maturity is not something we achieve, but something that occurs when the magnetic love of God draws together the diverse components of our lives in responsive love. The awesome grace of God captures our heart and mind and strength and brings them together in worship. To offer one's whole life to God is to be maturing; and to offer our mind is a part of that maturation.

WORDS AND MYSTERY

Theology puts our thoughts into words. We say what we think; words express our convictions. These expressions take many forms, hence we possess theological statements in the form of creeds (e.g., the Apostles' Creed), in books (e.g., Augustine's *Confessions* and John Wesley's *Sermons*), in scriptural and historical studies (e.g., biblical commentaries and biographies and histories of ideas), and in efforts at practical application (e.g., ethical formation and actions).

But all of our words, creeds, books, and statements—even all put together—are not completely adequate, as they do not say everything about God. God is mystery, and God's mystery is both the beginning point and the final assertion of theology. God is not a problem to be solved. We cannot know God exhaustively. Mystery remains mysterious. By our own efforts, we cannot probe the ultimate meaning of God. But God has revealed who God is, and before the Holy God we stand in awe and wonder, and attempt to respond if only with a stammerer's tongue.

Charles Wesley captures something of this sense of mystery and the inexpressible reality of God in his meditation on "Love Divine, All Loves Excelling." After struggling to say what he cannot say adequately (for God's love is not comparable to any other love), he closes by acknowledging that he is "Lost in wonder, love, and praise."

HUMBLE COURAGE

To speak of God at all requires both humility and courage. To be aware of God is to be overwhelmed. It is to be dumb struck (not talking may be the most appropriate act of respect). To know God is to know one cannot speak adequately about God; it is to know the impossibility of describing God in any complete way; it is to know that every theological statement falls short.

Yet we do speak. Indeed we must speak, but not to *capture* God, not to master God. Rather we speak because we have been claimed by a reality that draws words to our lips: words of rejoicing, of prayer, of reflection. We speak in response to our having been spoken to. God starts a dialogue; God speaks and we make, at least, a thankful and serious effort to respond.

For theology to undertake speaking about God expresses a love of truth. Theology is not an effort to possess the truth, to be in control of truth, or to be the speaker of the final truth. Rather, we speak of God because we have been possessed by truth and we want to be faithful to that truth. As believers, we are claimed by God, who is truth. We know God, yet only in part. We see, but only through a glass darkly. When we speak of God, we know that our words are inadequate; we point to truth, knowing that there is more truth than we have discovered. To attempt to speak theologically requires courage and humility. We need courage to say what we do understand of God; we need humility to say that we do not understand everything.

In the final part of Dante Alighieri's *The Divine Comedy, Paradiso,* Pope Gregory the Great is depicted as arriving in heaven. The great work of Gregory's life was to attempt to arrange the angels in order. To develop this scheme was his theological task and he wrote a big book on his studies. When Gregory arrived in heaven he looked around and realized his scheme was not accurate and he smiled.[2]

Gregory's effort is a parable of the good theologian. We work as hard as we can to understand theological issues. We use our spiritual and mental energies to do the work well. But if we find, in the end, that our effort has not captured all of the truth, we relax and smile. For beyond one's effort stands God's mystery, God's forgiveness, and God's renewing grace.

From beginning to end, theology is an offering of our life—including intellectual life—to God.

To think theologically is an utterly serious and an ultimately unfinished task. Heavy with thought, we are buoyed by grace. For God, who forgives our sins, also forgives our false ideas and our failure to comprehend as well as we should.

To speak of God is a great responsibility. Yet, to speak is necessary when God is central to our lives. With courage we speak, and with humility we know that God has the last word.

WHY THEOLOGY?

Let us press the issue directly: Whatever its general value, why should United Methodists be concerned about theology? Why should this be an issue at this time in our Church?

The answer is simple: Our beliefs shape who we are. In a time when self-identity is especially important (and difficult to state) among churches, to be clear about foundations of faith takes on great significance. To ask who are we as United Methodists calls for clarity of answer. We are people who believe and act and through our beliefs and actions offer our lives to God.

United Methodist traditions grew as they vigorously proclaimed the essentials of their faith. A clear and thoughtful proclamation of this faith continues to be a principal mission of the church.

AN INVITATION

This book is an invitation to become theologically aware; it is an invitation to begin a journey, a journey into faithful understanding. As Christian believers, we are already thinking about God, so the only questions are: Will we develop our thoughts faithfully and carefully? Will we develop an ability to communicate the reality of God?

CHAPTER II

Thinking About God

*W*e are all theologians. Theology is thinking about God and talking about God. But, more precisely, how does one actually do theology? How does theology work?

Is preaching a sermon doing theology? Is telling a story doing theology? Is singing an anthem doing theology? Sermons and many stories and anthems certainly contain theology. But they are alternate ways of describing God.

Two biblical passages can help illustrate the difference: The story of the prodigal son in Luke 15 and a series of statements in Ephesians 2:1-10. The story of the prodigal son is a story with which we can identify, a story that reminds people of a common experience of being lost and found. As a story, it presents a slice of human life. It is told in order to capture attention, to invite identification with the characters, and to convey truths about divine-human relationships.

In Ephesians 2 we have a theological discussion of the same issues of being lost and found. But the discussion takes the form of theological statements, not that of a story. Ephesians 2 is more abstract. The characteristic statements can fit any number of stories. What we have in these verses is a skeleton of ideas on which different stories or sermons might hang.

Read the story of the prodigal son, then look at the Ephesians passage.

First, the human condition is described: "You were dead through the trespasses and sins in which you once lived, following the course of this world" (Eph. 2:1-2). "We were by nature the children of wrath" (Eph. 2:3).

Second, God's grace is described: "But God, who is rich in mercy . . . made us alive together with Christ" (Eph. 2:4-5); "And raised us up with him . . . that . . . he might show the immeasurable riches of his grace. . . . For by grace you have been saved through faith, and this is not your own doing; it is the gift of God" (Eph. 2:6-8).

These verses illustrate a theological analysis. They present, in skeletal form, the issues of human sin, separation from God, and God's grace that renews relationship and thereby redeems and enhances human life. Most strongly stressed is God's freely given love (grace).

Upon this skeleton, any number of stories or sermons might be given shape. Think of the stories of the good Samaritan (seen as Christ) (Luke 10), the lost sheep and the lost coin (Luke 15), and Paul's conversion (Acts 9:1-9). Innumerable sermons on human sin and divine redemption can be and have been built on this one skeleton.

Theology attempts to make clear the ideas upon which a story or sermon is built. It also attempts to judge whether a particular story or sermon presents the basic ideas clearly—for instance, whether human sin is recognized as radical separation from God and whether God's free grace is given central attention. Some stories or sermons distort these truths. Primary elements might be neglected or wrongly presented. If so, one would say that the story, however well-intentioned, is not theologically sound.

Theology is to storytelling or preaching as engineering is to architecture. An architect (like a preacher or storyteller) presents a concept, a picture of a building. This presentation should be artistically attractive and useful for the purposes intended, such as the planning of a church structure or office building. The engineer then checks to see if the foundation is strong enough to hold the superstructure, whether stresses are dealt with, and whether the building has appropriate utility arrangements and can perform the functions planned for.

The task of theology is to check carefully to be sure that central emphases of Christian faith are clearly and appropriately made.

THE QUESTION OF TRUTH

To speak of central emphases of Christian faith is to say that there are emphases that should be made, emphases that Christian faith takes to be true.

But what is true? And what is truth?

The two questions are not exactly the same. God is true and God is truth. Jesus Christ is true and he is truth. To say that God in Jesus Christ is true is to say that God acts in accordance with God's own nature. Truth has to do with human understanding of God's true nature.

Our language about God is a reach for truth, an effort to express truth. But our language never fully grasps truth; our language can never claim to capture all of the truth about God, for God is mystery.

God is true and only God can speak the truth. And God has spoken in a person, in Jesus Christ. So, for Christian faith, truth is a person. Truth is Jesus Christ. In Jesus Christ, we are encountered by truth.

For Christians, true life is life set in true relation to God and neighbors; it is being grasped by the One who is true. True life sets the context for understanding the truth of God made known in Jesus Christ. From this perspective we discover truth.

Truth is what God in Scripture has said about God's nature. This truth is beyond our perfect grasp. But we also use the word *truth* to refer to human understanding of God, of ourselves, and of our world. This human truth is a reflection—and always a partial reflection—of God's expression of truth.

Christians, as human beings, love and worship God, who is true; we are attentive to God's truthful self-disclosure in Jesus Christ; and we make every effort to represent that truth in what we say about God. But, as humans, what we say about God is never fully equal to what God says of God's self.

Nevertheless, some human claims about God have special status as truthful interpretations of God. So we affirm the Apostles' Creed, the Nicene Creed, or Methodism's Articles of Religion. But even such official statements are not exhaustive—

they do not say everything about God. So we must be clear about the source of theological claims.

We can begin by saying that the foundation of truth, in Christian understanding, is *relational*. That is to say, it is based upon relationship with God.

Truth is a person and is known in personal relationship. Truth is not just an intellectual achievement. Truth grows out of true relationships. Truth also conveys an understanding that helps align one's life in a true manner with God.

Human descriptions of the divine/human relationship, of the one who initiates that relationship, and of implications of that relationship are attempts to state the truth. Such descriptions are important pointers to the truth that is Jesus Christ. The struggle to speak the truth are efforts to speak faithfully about God, who is truth, and who makes life true.

Some of our language is close to the center of accurate description. So to speak of God's free grace and unmerited favor has, over time, been taken to be a necessary way of talking about how God in Christ relates to human beings. Other issues, such as the exact character of human freedom or the nature of heaven, remain more in doubt and do not hold so essential a place.

Central to any theological description is the attempt to describe adequately God's self-presentation in Jesus Christ. This description is necessary in order to present Christ as accurately as possible. The task of theology is not to achieve a final description or to create an argument that is convincing to everyone.

The task of theology is to present Jesus Christ in such a way as to increase the possibility of relating to him and having life formed by him.

Theology provides a vital support for preaching and storytelling; it serves the presentation of the gospel; and it attempts to make that presentation authentic. Theology is not an end in itself. It is not a final goal of Christian understanding.

Theology attempts to help make the presentation of Jesus Christ as true as it can be so that encounter by him and with him will be as authentic as possible.

In the tradition of John Wesley, preaching is for the purpose of transforming life. Theology supports preaching by attempting to make the presentation of the gospel as authentic as possible. Theology intends to serve the transformation or the true alignment of life.

GUIDELINES

Are there guidelines for helping us find and speak the most basic truths of Christian understanding of God? The United Methodist tradition has said there are four such guidelines: Scripture, tradition, experience, and reason.

United Methodism is not unique in making these emphases, but it does consistently stress these themes in an attempt to make its theological claims truthful.

We shall later investigate each of these theological points of reference. For now, we want simply to mention the way they function as guides to truth.

Theology, we have said, helps us to speak truly about God. But theology does not develop out of nothing. Theology is not a free imaginative construction of our ideas of God and the world, or a creative attempt to show personal intelligence or intellectual acrobatics.

WHERE THEOLOGY BEGINS

Christian theology is an attempt to understand God's act in Jesus Christ. To speak theologically, in Christian terms, is to speak about who Jesus is, what Jesus has done, and what this says about God and about human beings.

The correct theological question is: What has God done in Jesus Christ? To question what God can do is never proper. If we ask about God's capabilities, the answer is always the same: anything.

To ask what God can do means that any answer is correct, for we are talking about infinite possibilities. Or we make ridiculous logic problems: Can God make a round square? Can God make a rock so big God can't pick it up? Too often we ask, "But can't God do that?" The question is improper.

The correct theological question is: What has God done? God has revealed God's own self. Theological reflection begins with those historic events, and not with human cunning or imagination. God, by God's initiative, is the source of our theological reflection; God speaks and we attempt to speak in response.

What has God done? This is the correct question for developing Christian theological interpretation. This question carries us to the Bible. In the scriptural accounts there are specific points of reference and controlling frameworks that shape our ideas.

Here is our first approach to the question: What has God done?

Through Scripture, we look to Jesus Christ. The story of Jesus is, of course, set within the tradition of the Old Testament. So we understand Jesus against the background of the Exodus, of God's covenant with the Hebrews, of the history of the Hebrew people, of the prophets, and of the Psalms and the wisdom books—such as Proverbs or Ecclesiastes. And the story of Jesus is explicitly set forth in the New Testament. In the books of the new covenant we discover what God has done.

In Jesus God is defined. In Jesus we are given God's fullest expression of grace—gracious judgment and redemption—and God's fullest exposure of the meaning of divine-human relationship. From this perspective, we develop understandings of such themes as God as creator, God as Holy Spirit, God as triune, and God as transformer of the world.

We have, in this discussion, placed emphasis on the centrality of Jesus Christ. This is the central core of theology in the Methodist tradition. Yet, to capture the full range of theological positions in Methodism, it is necessary to recognize that some theologians have more decisively stressed God as creator, the Holy Spirit, aspects of Christian experience, or the Trinity. The span of theological interest is wide, and there must be serious recognition of this diversity. Nevertheless, the stress on Jesus Christ as the central source of the knowledge of God is characteristic of this tradition.

HOW THEOLOGY DEVELOPS

United Methodist theology has claimed that we come to understand Jesus, his meaning and significance, primarily through the study of Scripture (where the story of Jesus is set in context and then told). To this source are added the study of tradition (where we have the accumulation of Christian reflection on Jesus), the investigation of Christians' experience of relationship with Jesus, and careful thought on all of these sources. (These guidelines will be discussed more carefully in chapter 7.)

We do not begin to think theologically with a blank mind or with no history. We are the inheritors of a rich tradition of presentations of Jesus, of sustained and faithful attempts to understand Jesus, of saints who have experienced the presence and meaning of Jesus, and of uncommonly talented minds that have reflected upon Jesus. We, as Christians, have been given much and we must use our inheritance.

Theology has a historical base; it is reflection upon God's action in history. Theology is not abstract speculation; rather, it is an effort to understand the concrete encounters of God with humankind and especially as this is expressed in Jesus Christ. And theology attempts to pursue the implications of God's action for the full range of life.

Theology intends to serve the establishing and enhancement of relationships between God and persons. Theology does not so much attempt merely to interpret the world; theology attempts to serve the transformation of human life, the formation of

Christian community, and through this the reformation of human society.

Insofar as intellectual issues are involved in the transformation of life, theology must deal with them. So theology discusses issues like what it means to be chosen and what it means to be free, the relation of a good God to the realities of evil, and the differences between providence—as God's willful guidance—and fate as determinism. But these issues are discussed, not to offer abstract intellectual solutions, but in order to understand how they fit into themes of grace, redemption, and hope.

We try to think theologically so that we can better fulfill our mission to preach the gospel and share its benefits with God's world.

Theology is for the purpose of helping us think clearly about God. We think best by going to the place where God has spoken most clearly about God's self—that is, in Jesus Christ. We are guided in this effort by Scripture, tradition, experience, and reason.

Sir Herbert Butterfield, an eminent British historian and Methodist lay preacher, concludes his discussion of the dynamics of modern history in his book, *Christianity and History*, with the sentence, "We can do worse than remember a principle which both gives us a firm rock and leaves us the maximum elasticity for our minds, the principle: Hold to Christ, and for the rest be totally uncommitted."[3]

A basic theological principle in the Wesleyan tradition is: Keep clear about the center. In response to Jesus Christ, who has claimed us, hold fast to that Christ. Keep the center firm. One then has liberty to consider all other things and keep them in proper perspective.

CHAPTER III

Theological Discussion in United Methodism

Every church possesses a theological tradition; every church has present theological activities. So United Methodism possesses a tradition and constantly undertakes fresh theological statement. *The Discipline of The United Methodist Church* sets all of this forth in "Our Doctrinal Heritage," "Our Doctrinal History," and "Our Theological Task." These discussions can be found in *The Discipline* (1988) in paragraphs 66-69 (pp. 40-90).[4]

But in order to approach the theological statements in *The Discipline* we need to make some introductory comments. We need to understand who speaks for United Methodism in terms of doctrine (which will be defined shortly), how theological exploration (which will also be defined) takes place, and how tradition is maintained and how new ideas are approved.

GENERAL CONFERENCE

In United Methodism, General Conference (the elected, governing body of United Methodism that meets every four years) alone possesses the authority to speak for the Church in terms of doctrine. Neither the Council of Bishops nor any other church assembly has this power. The General Conference, in session, may take any action it considers appropriate in regard to the doctrines of the church (the one exception is that it may not change the Articles of Religion or the Confession of Faith which, by constitution, may not be altered).[5]

At General Conference, the statements of belief may be considered and changes made for inclusion in *The Discipline.* For example, at General Conference in 1988 a committee on "Faith and Mission" reworked the theological section that had been written in 1972—just after the creation of The United Methodist Church by the union of The Methodist Church and the Evangelical United Brethren in 1968. This new statement now constitutes paragraphs 66-69 in the 1988 *Discipline.*

The fact that General Conference has this authority says something significant about United Methodist theology: It is worked out through discussion among clergy and laity. This type of theological work and decision-making is called *conciliar theology.* Conciliar theology means that there is no authority—of priests or laity—that decides on doctrine and then passes it down to others. Rather, an elected body (which changes regularly) is continually responsible for interpreting the faith of The United Methodist Church.

A CASE IN POINT

As an illustration of conciliar theology, consider how the 1988 statement came into being. In 1984,

General Conference appointed a commission to restudy the then current theological statement and to report the commission's finding to the 1988 General Conference.[6] The study group was representative of the membership of United Methodism and spent three years in careful preparation of the document to be submitted.

At General Conference, a legislative committee of more than ninety persons reworked the submitted report. This committee presented its revision to the full conference membership. The document was approved by a vote of over 90 percent. The dynamics of the discussions both in the commission and the legislative committee revealed the intensity and the spirit of the encounters.

In order to enter into discussion of the theological statement in the 1988 *Discipline,* it will be helpful to discuss an important distinction within the document—the distinction between doctrinal affirmation and theological exploration.

DOCTRINAL AFFIRMATION AND THEOLOGICAL EXPLORATION

Within the broad frame of theology we can distinguish between doctrine and theological exploration. On the one hand, doctrinal statements (or doctrinal standards) represent the agreement of the church at a given time about its faith. On the other hand, theological reflection leads in the exploration of fresh interpretations of faith. A creed accepted by a church is a doctrine; the writings of a particular theologian are exploratory theology. So, the Articles of Religion or the Confession of Faith are church doctrines (see *The Discipline,* pp. 53-77), while the writings of a United Methodist theologian are exploratory theology.

Doctrine reflects the grasp of the Church; theological exploration reflects the reach of the Church. To use another analogy: Doctrine is the part of the cathedral already completed, exploratory theology is creative architectural vision and preliminary drawings for possible new construction.

The relation of doctrine and exploratory theology is complex—each requires the other. In our present context, exploration usually follows doctrine, yet doctrine can also follow exploration. Each can give rise to the other.

Doctrine is the declaration of the collective understanding of the Church expressed in agreed-upon formulations such as creeds. The Church, responsive to the leadership of the Holy Spirit, makes—and the Church may amend—doctrine. But, until the Church amends it, a doctrinal statement is the historical property of the Church and may function as Doctrinal Standards, that is, as the official position of the church.[7]

Doctrine is basic to the Church's existence, therefore the development of doctrine is a primary obligation of the Church. The Church, by its doctrine, protects itself from the fantastic, the erroneous, and the superstitious (such as from the work of astrologers). Doctrine provides for the well-being of the Church, and it is a special privilege of the Church to develop its doctrinal standards.

A dimension of the Church's attempt to express its faith is in its exploratory work. Theological exploration is doctrine in the making; it is doctrine stretched in new directions. Exploration is theology expressing the Church's reach.

Before the Church can make new communal confession(s) of doctrines, long periods of theological exploration, of freedom, and of maturation are required. This effort is theology as trial and error. Theological exploration is built upon and nurtured by doctrine, but it utilizes its freedom in Christ through the Holy Spirit to critique doctrine and to search for new ways of expressing the Christian faith.

Exploratory theology is an authentic expression of the Church's life. If the Church's life is full and free, its theological exploration will be rich and growing, fresh and freshly invigorating. Doctrine is the communal property of the Church; but the work of individuals in reflection, criticism, and exploration shapes that communal property.

Combining these elements can be risky, but a tradition that does not allow for serious self-criticism and the freedom of exploration stops the growth of faith. At the same time, a tradition that does not acknowledge the corporate dimension of faith in doctrinal fashion stunts the life of creative community. Exploratory theology is usually the work of an individual, but it gains its worth only by way of the individual theologian's connection to the community of the Church. New insights arise from tradition and are a part of tradition, for tradition is kept alive by the new understandings of those who carry it into the future.

Exploration is significant only if it affects the life of the Church. Explorers who simply go on exploring, but never come home or report their findings do not make a contribution. Exploratory theology, to be important, must share its findings with the community of the Church. The results may not be accepted; or they may be used for further exploration; or they may be affirmed and made a part of Church doctrine. Whatever the case, the Church, as a community, must act in order for exploratory theology to become doctrine.

Both doctrine and exploratory theology are crucial to the health and life of the Church; their most vibrant expressions are found within the community of faith. The theological paragraphs in *The Discipline* call for the entire Body of Christ — both laity and clergy (the conciliar group) — to be engaged in study. Such study supports the continuing vitality of faith within the Church.

Theological exploration and doctrinal affirmation belong in the Church. They are the Church's offering of its mind — along with its will, its affections, and its service — to God. The community of faith must be theologically engaged in order to nourish its life and mission.

PUTTING IT TOGETHER

Let's take several giant steps and put in skeletal form what we said in the first two chapters and how that fits with this third chapter. We made several major points:

All people who talk about God are theologians;
Our theological statements accept God as mystery;
With humility and courage we attempt to be responsible in our speech about God;
God is true and truth; our words reflect God's truth, always in partial ways;

To guide our thought we use the guidelines of Scripture,
   tradition, experience, and reason;
In this third chapter, we have described the role of
   General Conference (which affirms theology as a com-
   munity enterprise), as well as the distinction between
   Doctrine and Exploratory Theology.

United Methodism reflects all of these points.

We assume that everyone in the Church should
be attempting to come to a clearer understanding
of God—the entire body of Christ is involved. This
is a conciliar form of theology; that is, one that
includes all believers.

United Methodists affirm their faith in a variety
of ways. We share much with other Christians and
we have some distinctive positions of our own (we
shall explore these points more fully in subsequent
chapters). In any event, we are sharply aware that
no theological formulation is final. God is mystery.
The fact that no theology is final requires ongoing
theological study in the Church.

Consequently, as a Church we struggle to state
the truth. The final responsibility for this statement
is given to General Conference, and General
Conference places its theological decisions in *The
Discipline* and other documents officially adopted
by the General Conference.

The first theological task of General Conference
is to define Doctrinal Standards. The second theological task is to encourage exploratory theology. An
ongoing theological task is to consider exploratory
theology for its possible contribution to Church
doctrine.

The theological effort of General Conference
works within the guidelines of Scripture, tradition,
experience, and reason (guidelines that are them-

selves the result of exploratory theology). The use of these guidelines provides a thoroughly Methodist character to this consideration.

Through the interaction of doctrine and exploratory theology, we attempt to be faithful in our theology and, thereby, to present the gospel authentically.

CHAPTER IV

Acknowledging Our Heritage

What do United Methodists believe? It is to our Doctrinal Standards that we refer for the answers. We turn now to these central doctrines.

The first major section of *The Discipline* (pp. 40-78) contains the Doctrinal Statement of United Methodism. These doctrines are the foundations of the United Methodist expression of the Christian faith. A glance through these pages in *The Discipline* will be helpful in building a sense of the theological emphases that make up the house of faith in which we live.

In developing the Doctrinal Standards that United Methodists affirm, *The Discipline* makes two preliminary moves: It acknowledges a broad and rich heritage of the Christian faith in general, and it sets forth Methodism's distinctive doctrinal history. In this chapter, we shall set forth our wider Christian heritage,[8] and in the next chapter we will turn to the distinctive characteristics of United Methodist belief.

A COMMON FAITH

"United Methodists share a common heritage with Christians of every age and nation" (p. 41). This affirmation indicates the deep roots and the broad sympathies of our Church. We are Christians and are pleased to acknowledge that our faith is shared with other Christians.

United Methodists claim neither a unique possession of Christian faith nor an unwillingness to recognize our indebtedness to other Christians. All we do is claim that we have a way of affirming Christian belief that has come by a particular route, a route we shall follow in the next chapter.

John Wesley believed that the things that bind Christians together are more important than the things that separate them. United Methodists also affirm this and so affirm the catholic or basic faith of all Christians. In contemporary language, this means we are *ecumenical*—we hold hands with all people who share a common faith in Jesus Christ.

Further, we know there is much to be learned from other Christians. Christian truth is too large for any single body of believers—including United Methodists—to control. The special angles and distinctive perspectives of different Christians enrich all others. We want and need to be open to others who are followers of the way. We affirm the holy catholic church.

The text of the disciplinary statement (pp. 40-44) should be read carefully and taken to mean what it says. The opening paragraph is crafted precisely.

United Methodists profess the historic Christian faith in God, incarnate in Jesus Christ for our salvation and ever at work in human history in the Holy Spirit. Living in a covenant of grace under the Lordship of Jesus Christ, we participate in the first fruits of God's coming reign and pray in hope for its full realization on earth as in heaven (p. 40).

Central doctrines of Christian faith follow. What we hold in common with other Christians is spelled out; there are seven primary emphases (pp. 42-44). We confess:

—belief in the triune God—Father, Son, and Holy Spirit;
—a faith in the mystery of salvation in and through Jesus Christ;
—God's redemptive love as realized in human life by the activity of the Holy Spirit, both in personal experience and in the community of believers;
—to be part of Christ's universal Church when by adoration, proclamation, and service we become conformed to Christ;
—that the reign of God is both a present and future reality;
—the authority of Scripture in matters of faith, justification by grace through faith, and recognition that the Church is in need of continual reformation and renewal;
—the essential oneness of the Church of Jesus Christ.

A typical way of summing up United Methodist understanding of its place in the wider Christian community is to say we are:

truly catholic,
truly evangelical,
truly reformed.

Truly catholic points to our heritage in the larger Christian tradition; we align ourselves with all those throughout the ages who are aligned with Jesus Christ.

Truly evangelical points to our emphases on the gospel, on the centrality of grace, and on personal conversion.

Truly reformed indicates our conviction that the Church must undergo continual renewal and be constantly vigilant about its faithfulness to God.

CREEDS WE SHARE

Within the statement of our common heritage we find reference to "ecumenical creeds"—namely, the Apostles' Creed, the Nicene Creed, and the Chalcedonian definition.

The creeds originated as texts used in worship— as what we now call the profession of faith in the baptismal covenant. They are not abstract, speculative statements about God. They were formulated as concrete descriptions of God as we know God in the relationship we enter through baptism.

The Apostles' Creed was initially formulated for this purpose in the second or third century in Rome, but did not reach its final form until about A.D. 650. This baptismal statement of faith grew and developed until eventually it gave expression to the faith of Western Christians. This creed does not encompass all Christian truth or all that is involved in a thoughtful understanding of God. But it does, in a concise manner, express basic Christian convictions about God, Jesus Christ, and the Holy Spirit. We do not need to rush to establish new doctrinal standards, but may follow faithfully the pace of the Holy Spirit.

What we know as the Nicene Creed is based on the baptismal covenant of one of the Eastern churches. This became the basis of the consensus reached by the ecumenical church at the Councils of Nicaea and Constantinople in the fourth century and received as a statement of the churches' faith by Christians throughout the world. That is the reason that it begins "We believe," not "I believe."

In a period of less than one hundred and fifty years (A.D. 325–451) the church reached consensus on central elements of its faith. This century was a time of enormous energy due to political controversy, changes in the Roman empire, conflicts among the churches, and unusual intellectual effort.

Coming out of this time of turmoil, the church held three councils: Nicaea (325), Constantinople (381), and Chalcedon (451). These councils firmly established the basic understanding of the person of Jesus Christ and made clear the central elements of trinitarian Christianity (fuller discussion of the Holy Spirit would follow, but the ingredients for completing the doctrine of the Trinity were now in place).

To say that United Methodists understand these creeds to be foundational is to say, as the theological statement does, "These statements of faith . . . contain the most prominent features of our ecumenical heritage" (p. 41).

THE LIMITS OF CREEDS

Creeds are important, but not final; they present basic truth, but they do not exhaust Christian teaching. Creeds represent the corporate faith of Christian community at a given time. To say creeds are basic to a tradition is not to say they are complete in themselves. Creeds do point back to Scripture. Creeds have a history of interpretation, and they are springboards for theological exploration that attempts to make the gospel relevant to new situations.

A New Testament scholar once commented that for Paul to say what Jesus said, Paul had to say the same thing differently. We can add that for contemporary Christians to say what the Apostles' Creed, the Nicene Creed, or the Chalcedonian definition said, we must find fresh ways to repeat their grasp of truth.

The creeds do not stop Christian theological reflection, they promote it. Creeds are important as they point beyond themselves to Scripture, and through Scripture to God in Jesus Christ. Creeds do not restrict our thought, rather they set directions and guidelines. Creeds are important markers along the way of Christian reflection on God, and they represent important points of consensus in the church.

FAMILIAR BUT IMPORTANT THEMES

In this chapter we have moved quickly through some of the most important themes in Christian doctrine. These themes are familiar. So familiar in fact, that we sometimes fail to appreciate their true importance.

With swift movement we have referred to God as triune, to salvation and redemptive love, to the church and the reign (kingdom) of God, and to the authority of Scripture.

Now let us move more slowly, look back at these themes and attempt to refind their significance. In these few statements are some of the most basic claims Christians make.

We are not attempting to look deeply or thoroughly at particular doctrines. Rather, we are attempting to set a framework for doing theology and suggesting ways to develop theology. The books that follow in this series probe some doctrines in depth. So the reading of this book should be followed by study of the next volumes. We need, however, to look briefly at these central themes in order to set them in context.

We believe in the triune God—Father, Son, and Holy Spirit. This affirmation is uniquely Christian. God is triune, three in one. Christians do not believe in one God, then add Christ and the Holy Spirit. The God Christians worship is always and irreducibly three in one.

The words *Father, Son,* and *Holy Spirit* name our God. God is the sovereign source of all creation and of our lives. God, the first person, is also One who expresses love, who hears prayers, and who cares intimately for all creation.

The person Jesus Christ is the embodiment of God's love, the word and grace of God, humankind's redeemer—the One who is the way, the truth, and the life. Here we are at the heartland of Christian faith and we must say as accurately as possible who Jesus is.

The person of the Holy Spirit is God's immediate presence. God, as Spirit, is universally present: There is no place where God is not, no time when

God is not, no one with whom God is not present. The Holy Spirit communes with human spirits to recreate and nurture relationships.

Familiarity can breed contempt; it can also breed simple oversight. To mention these themes of Father, Son, and Holy Spirit seems common to Christians. But how awesome it is to speak of God in these ways! Here is the center of our faith, the basis of our lives, the meaning of our existence, and the ground of our hope.

These claims are so central that they define what Christian faith means, what it means to be Christian. Over the centuries Christian churches have given primary place to these doctrines. Here, as perhaps nowhere else, we know what we must say and we know how inadequate our language is.

We affirm that we worship the Trinity. But no creed can capture all of God's truth, no portrait is adequate to depict Jesus Christ, and no verse or experience can contain the Holy Spirit. Yet we also know that here, in this triune God (which is a developed theological theme), we are touching on the central meaning and mystery of our lives.

So also with the other great themes we share with other Christians. Themes such as the redemption of life, reestablishing of positive relationship with God, and the finding of new being in God.

In addition, church doctrine has stressed that in Christian existence we become a part of the body of Christ, the community of the church. This becoming is not simply a gathering of completely separate individuals, it is a binding of life, a sharing of sorrow and joy, a living together, and a serving together. New being is found in communal existence with Jesus Christ and other believers.

Further, the reign or kingdom of God sets the context of our present existence in the body of Christ. This doctrine also states our hope for the future—when God will be all in all, when the kingdoms of this world shall become the kingdom of our God and of Christ and of the Holy Spirit.

We mention these themes, all too quickly, to indicate how important these doctrines, held in common by Christians, actually are. These beliefs constitute the foundation of the Church; they represent the basic consensus among Christians.

The first thing it means for United Methodists to do theology is to begin to think about, to reflect on, and to probe more deeply these basic doctrines.

CHAPTER V

United Methodist Distinctives

*E*merging from the rich background shared with most Christians is an inner circle of doctrines especially important in the traditions that come together in United Methodism. In this chapter we will concentrate on doctrinal affirmations; in the next chapter we will consider theological explorations. The original doctrines in Methodism derive chiefly from John Wesley, who was the originator of the Methodist revival movement in eighteenth-century England. Wesley is the fountainhead of Methodist theological self-understanding.

The following emphases represent doctrine within United Methodism. *The Discipline* mentions the following six special emphases (pp. 46-48):

> —prevenient grace;
> —justification and assurance;
> —sanctification and perfection;
> —faith and good works;
> —mission and service;
> —nature and mission of the church.

In addition, the disciplinary statement emphasizes some other characteristics of Methodism. It highlights the relation of doctrine and discipline in the Christian life, especially as they are expressed in early Methodism's General Rules and in ongoing Methodism's Social Principles (pp. 49-50).

PRACTICAL DIVINITY

To appreciate the distinctive character of United Methodism's theological life, faith and practice must be held tightly together. Indeed, for the Wesleyan tradition, to believe is to live according to one's convictions—faith and action cannot be separated.

According to John Wesley, theology is important insofar as it produces transformed living and supports the growth of Christian maturity. Theology is not an intellectual activity separated from the rest of life; theology is a part of Christian existence and is important because it helps us learn who God is and who we are, we who respond to God in love and service. This is what Wesley meant by *practical divinity.*

To press the matter further, theology is not first developed and then applied. It is precisely in interaction with practice that interpretation (theology, theory) develops. Theological understanding is expressed in transformed living—in life reflecting the mind of Christ—and transformed living provides substance to theological understanding.

Theology helps develop transformed living; Christian living helps shape Christian understanding. To have faith in God is to love God and to serve God; to love God is to come to an understanding of

God and to serve God; to serve God is to love God and to have an understanding of God. Everything is tied together.

Perhaps the statement of Jesus in the Fourth Gospel best brings these together. "I am the way, and the truth, and the life" (John 14:6). *The Imitation of Christ,* a devotional study much admired by John Wesley, comments on this. "Without that way there is no going, without that truth there is no knowing, without that life there is no living" (Book III, Chapter LVI). One might also add, in a Wesleyan manner: Without that way there is no knowing; without that truth there is no living; without that life there is no going.

DISTINCTIVE DOCTRINES

Christian life and thought are expressed in the distinctive doctrines that center in grace.

Prevenient Grace

For John Wesley all of life is graced, because grace is God present and God is present everywhere and to everyone. Grace is the central theme in Wesley's theology.

The word *prevenient* is archaic, the closest contemporary use we have is *preventive* medicine—that is, medicine that prevents serious disease, that which goes before, that which happens first. God acts first; it is God's character as grace to always take the initiative.

God's beginning comes before our beginning; God's future goes beyond our goals. God stands on both ends of life. Before we seek God, God has been seeking us. "We love because he first loved us" (I John 4:19). God also is ahead of us; God awaits us around every corner. Life begins, continues, and ends in God.

The highest Christian claims are: All is of God, and God is all grace.

Justification and Assurance (Justifying Grace)

For John Wesley, justification by grace through faith is God's forgiveness that calls us to gratitude. Actual Christian existence begins at this point, for justification presupposes that human beings are separated from God and must be brought back into right relationship with God.

God reaches across the divide; it is God who forgives and calls for decisive change in human love. We who rebel are nevertheless, by grace, called children by God and may live in new covenant with God (to respond to God is conversion into new life).

To be justified is to be set in right relationship: Life is adjusted to God, moved toward alignment with God's will, and brought into community with God. This alignment is what we mean by transformed living.

Assurance—that is, to be sure of our relationship with God—is to hear the Holy Spirit say "You are God's child." And it is to believe in and act on these words. Assurance is confidence in God, in God's prevenient grace, and God's establishing new relationship; it is not to be confident about the strength of our faith or the strength of our faithfulness. Assurance is God's word to us, not our word to God.

In terms of assurance, John Wesley believed that human beings can know God's love with such confidence that they do not have simply to hope, or wait to see what God will do, or to find out after death if God's love is secure. In present experience, God's love may be counted on and we can say that we are securely held by God's love.

With Paul, we can affirm, "For I am convinced that neither death, nor life, nor angels, nor rulers, nor things present, nor things to come, nor powers, nor height, nor depth, nor anything else in all creation, will be able to separate us from the love of God in Christ Jesus our Lord" (Rom. 8:38-39).

Sanctification and Perfection (Sanctifying Grace)

No words are more characteristic of John Wesley's theology than *sanctification* and *perfection*. Yet, none are more difficult to make clear.

Sanctification means "to be made holy," and *perfection* means "to love God with all one's heart and mind and strength" (Matt. 22:37 paraphrase). Yet, our constant sense is that we are not holy or pure and that our love of God is so often feeble. Was Wesley taking a hopelessly optimistic view of Christian life?

John Wesley certainly knew temptations: to worship false gods, to turn from God even after one had turned to God, to give God only a part of our love, our mind, or our service. Nevertheless, Wesley believed that God's prevenient grace is always present, always drawing us toward God, always inciting us to love God more fully.

Wesley's prayer, which he repeated regularly in his Anglican worship, "that we may perfectly love Thee," is his expression of the Christian desire "to will one Thing," "to love God only," "to abandon life completely to God," "to simplify our lives by singular focus," and "to have no other god before our God."

The holy life, in Methodist tradition, is to find whole life. Life reaches for completeness as it is drawn together around God; all of life is focused on God. The goal of life is to let God be God.

Wesley sometimes spoke of people who did love God completely—though they were few in number. At other times he spoke of growing in grace, of perfect love as a process of growth.

Perhaps the best example of this relationship is a good friendship. Good friendship does not conclude a relationship. Friendship is an expanding experience; the better the friendship, the more life is opened for greater participation in friendship. So the love of God enriches the possibilities of divine-human relationship. To love God with all of our heart and soul and mind is to open ourselves to the endless possibilities of God's love and human response.

Sanctification and perfection come from gracious relationship; they are not achieved. The words of the hymn have the order correct: "Breathe on me breath of God, until my heart is pure." The theme of sanctification, of Christian holiness, of disciplined love of God and neighbor, is a central and distinctive emphasis of the Methodist tradition. Recovery of this theme is crucial for the ongoing life of our church.

Faith and Good Works

In the Wesleyan tradition, faith and good works cannot be separated. To have faith is to say Amen to what God has said about us; it is to trust life to God. Faith is not simply rational conviction, it is a way of life.

Faith is response to God that expresses the dynamic of the divine-human relationship; to be in this relationship is to live in awareness of and in faithfulness to the gracious God. Good works— works of Christlikeness—are motivated and given their special character because of our faith or trust in God. A double emphasis is formed. We love *because* God loves us, we love *in the way* God loves us.

Christian faith includes trust in God, which results in knowledge of God and in living with God. Christian actions are good when they reflect the character of Jesus Christ, and actions reflect the character of Jesus Christ when we are formed by him in his likeness.

For our Methodist tradition, transformation into the likeness of Christ is the goal of preaching, the goal of teaching, the goal of worship, and the goal of service. Belief without changed life is empty; efforts to be what we do not believe are futile.

The Nature and Mission of the Church

God calls the church into being. Christian community is formed by God's offer of covenant and the accepting response of human gratitude. Methodism stresses the establishing of the church through prevenient grace, justification, sanctification, and the life of faithful service. Methodism has also stressed that to be in relation with God places Christians in a special relation with other people—in close community with other Christians and in gracious mission to the world. The church is called to worship God and is sent to serve God.

There is emphasis on the reality of Christian community. To be Christian is to be in the body of Christ, to worship and live together with other Christians. Christian community is not an addition to Christian life, it is essential to Christian existence. To live with God and other Christians makes life whole. The church is the community of those who are in community with Jesus Christ; marks of the church are the true preaching of the word, the administration of the sacraments, fellowship, and mission.

In Methodism, mission is given special importance. To be bound to Christ is to be bound to the world; the world is to be loved as Christ has loved us. The gospel received is to be shared. Again, faith and works are bound together; again, practical divinity is the goal.[9]

Emphasis on conversion and the beginning of Christian life led Methodism to reduce to a minimum the vows of church membership:

(1) To confess Jesus Christ as Lord and Savior and pledge allegiance to his kingdom;

(2) To receive and profess the Christian faith as contained in the Scriptures of the Old and New Testaments;

(3) To promise to live a Christian life and remain faithful members of Christ's holy Church;

(4) To be loyal to The United Methodist Church and uphold it by prayer, presence, gifts, and service (pp. 124-25).

United Methodism's Summaries of Faith

The Articles of Religion of the Methodist Church (pp. 60-68) and the Confession of Faith of the Evangelical United Brethren Church (pp. 68-74) are tightly drawn summary statements of doctrines that provide the theological foundation of United Methodism. We find summaries of previous emphases in "Our Doctrinal Heritage" (pp. 40-50) and "Our Doctrinal History" (pp. 50-59). As with many summaries, these articles are more enduring in terms of what they affirm than in what they deny. The affirmations state the basic doctrines that we have been discussing in chapters 4 and 5.

The denials are dated and arise from controversies. For instance, in the Articles of Religion, after making ten affirmations, which continue to retain their importance, five denials of Roman Catholic positions are inserted: works done over and above God's commands, purgatory, communion only with bread, the uncompleted work of Jesus Christ, and the necessity of an unmarried ministry. The Confession of Faith of the EUB church—written some 150 years later—does not include these rejections, which shows how every theological statement, in part, reflects its own historical setting.

When, however, United Methodists are asked to give the essence of their doctrines, the Articles of Religion and the EUB Confession are important points of reference. But they do not contain all of the distinctive beliefs of United Methodists. The primary themes remain: prevenient grace, justification and assurance, sanctification and perfection, faith and good works, mission and service, and the nature and mission of the church.

Do United Methodists have theology? Emphatically, yes! Look at our distinctive emphases. They say what we believe.

DOCTRINE AND DISCIPLINE

We end this survey by returning to the initial emphasis: doctrine and life, theology and ethics, and beliefs and practice are always bound together. To believe in God is to live by the grace of God and to live graciously.

Illustrations of such character are found in the General Rules (pp. 74-77), which represent the earliest phase in Methodism, and the Social Principles (pp. 91-111), which represent current United Methodist effort to apply faithfully the gospel in contemporary life. Both of these statements point to the conscious attempt to embody faith.

This section of the theological statement closes with a summary sentence. "These distinctive emphases of United Methodists provide the basis for 'practical divinity,' the experiential realization of the gospel of Jesus Christ in the lives of Christian people" (p. 50).

CHAPTER VI

Our Theological Task

*I*n Section 4 of *The Discipline* (pp. 79-90), we move into different terrain. The Doctrinal Standards of United Methodism have been stated; our foundation has been put into place. Now there is fresh territory to be explored. We can now attempt to build on our established foundation for present interpretation.

The more secure the foundations, the more adventuresome new exploration can be. To move into new terrain it is not necessary to reject one's home base. But adventurous spirits often move beyond home to investigate larger arenas. Frontiers beckon. New challenges demand new response. Pioneers move from home into new surroundings; but they can take beliefs and values from home to sustain them on their journeys.

In Section 4 we move into theological exploration. In the last chapter we focused on doctrinal affirmations, now we turn to our present theological task. (Remember the distinction in chapter 3 between doctrinal affirmation and theological exploration.) In this exploration "our theological task includes the testing, renewal, elaboration, and application of our doctrinal perspective in carrying out our calling 'to spread scriptural holiness over these lands' " (p. 78).

How is such a task carried out? The statement in *The Discipline* suggests four characteristics of current theological work. We shall look at these in order.

CHARACTERISTIC TASKS

Critical and Constructive (p. 78)

Theology is Christian faith in its self-critical stance. That is, theology explores the foundations of faith, checks the logic of faith, investigates questions put to faith, looks at faith in a particular intellectual context, and even asks, why believe?

Doubt is not the opposite of faith; faith lives with doubt and lives facing doubt honestly. Faith takes doubt into its affirmation. The opposite of faith is unbelief or faithlessness. Because doubts do arise; faith must confront this reality—both to answer the doubts and to enrich its own life.

To have faith is not to live with absolute certainty, so that no questions ever arise. Faith is affirmation of a relationship, and, as with all good relationships, we live in confidence and not in security.

Faith is the courage to affirm meaning even when faced by threat; to have faith is to stand trustingly, sometimes with trembling trust, even when the earth shakes.

Theology is faith reflecting on itself; it sets forth the source, the significance, and the future of faith.

Sometimes theology questions, sometimes it manifests joy, sometimes it is rigorous rational inquiry, sometimes it stands on the boundary between faith and unbelief, sometimes it asks how faith relates to scientific belief or social or economic status.

Theology may be expressed in positive and constructive ways. Constructive theology is the effort to give new expression to Christian faith, especially to aspects that seem to have special importance at the present time. So theology may attempt to restate the doctrines of the Trinity, Christology, or the Holy Spirit. These doctrines must be restated to keep them fresh. Theology may attempt to rethink models of God that include feminine characteristics, liberation themes, or ecological sensitivities.

Constructive theology accepts the fact that pressing questions are being addressed to Christian faith and it responds to these questions with efforts to build better expressions of our faith for the present time.

Individual and Communal (pp. 78-79)

Contemporary Western culture has greatly stressed individualism and the special importance of individuals. Individuals have consequently been lifted out of communities and treated as free and rational beings who independently make their own rules and set their own goals. This emphasis on individuals has resulted in a loss of a sense of family and community; and persons are separated from their natural environment.

The Christian understanding of existence encompasses both God's affirmation of persons as uniquely important and persons in community. Christian life is life within the body of Christ; it is life that is found precisely in new-formed community (covenant). Family and community are not fortunate additions to essential personhood; they are the conditions that make personhood possible.

Contemporary theology is rediscovering that thought and interpretation, critical reflection and constructive effort are all communal activities. Indeed, theological vocabulary, our questions and answers, all arise within community and feed back into community. In contemporary theological work neither the contribution of individuals nor the communal context is to be isolated from the other, each lives in and out of the other. This, of course, is why we can and should speak of United Methodist theology.

No theologian is self-made; no theologian stands apart from a church community; no theologian speaks only for herself. Rather, all of us are inheritors of communal traditions, all of us have been nurtured in particular forms of worship, learning, serving, and thinking. So theology takes place in community and for community.

Even the greatest genius does not start from ground zero. Rather, he or she is shaped by the Christian communal culture and speaks from and to that community. (A church is also shaped by its own social environment and lives in relation to that environment.)

To say that the task of theology is both individual and communal is not to state two different things, it is to state two sides of the same coin, two dimensions of a single reality.

Contextual and Incarnational

All theology is concrete. Theology is written or spoken for a particular situation. Theology is self-deluded if it claims not to reflect a concrete society or racial or gender sensibilities. Abstract theology is impossible, and if it were possible it would be irrelevant.

Theology is bound to particular times, places, and circumstances. Rather than decry this condition, we should rejoice that the gospel has concrete relevance, that it speaks to actual women and men in actual social settings with special needs and hopes.

God's coming in Jesus Christ was historical. Jesus was a historical human being who was nurtured in a specific Hebrew tradition, in a specific place and town and country, within a particular political and economic order. He had particular companions, he died under Pontius Pilate and he, on the third day, rose from the dead.

So specific is all Christian existence. And just so specific is all Christian reflection on God. The theological task is, as *The Discipline* states, "contextual" and "incarnational." Since John Wesley was committed to a theology that issued in the transformation of life, it is concrete life, lived in concrete settings, which is transformed. United Methodist theology undertakes its theology from this perspective.

Practical

This theme states again what we have attempted to say throughout our discussion. For United

Methodists, as followers of John Wesley, theology is not an abstract, speculative, intellectual undertaking. Rather, theology serves life; it attempts to clarify and present God's good news as redemptive for persons, as formative of new community and as a challenge to social order.

In John Wesley's *Christian Library,* a series of fifty volumes, all but two of the volumes are biographies of exemplary Christians. Wesley was little interested in theological speculation, rather he attempted to present "plain truth for plain people" in order to lead them into mature Christian living.

UNITED METHODIST DIVERSITY

The above characteristics of our present theological task set a general stage on which United Methodist theology usually takes place. But to share a common stage is not to perform the theological task in a common manner. In fact, United Methodist theology is immensely diverse and represents a broad spectrum of present-day Christian interpretation.

To describe contemporary United Methodist theology is to cover most options found in contemporary Protestant theology.

This range is typical of Methodism. Methodist theology has always been sensitive to its cultural setting and has been receptive to what is going on within other Christian traditions. Also, distinctive Wesleyan emphases have worn many garments, so the same framework can take on different clothing and remain authentic. Wesleyan emphases tend to function more as internal energizers of theology than as outside boundaries. What kinds of theology have these energies produced?

United Methodist theologians have developed and expanded nineteenth- and twentieth-century Protestant themes in exploring the nature of faith and the philosophical understanding of God (John B. Cobb, Jr., Robert Neville, and Schubert M. Ogden), Wesleyan theology (Albert C. Outler, Robert E. Cushman, Thomas A. Langford), classical orthodox theology (Thomas C. Oden), evangelical theology (Ted A. Campbell), communal and character formation (Stanley Hauerwas), liberation themes (Theodore Runyon, Douglas M. Meeks, Theodore Jennings), feminist theology (Rebecca Chopp), Black theology (Major Jones), theology and culture (Manfred Marquardt), and ecumenical theology (John Deschner). In the wider Methodist family we find a theology of worship (Geoffrey Wainwright), Black theology (James H. Cone), theology of evangelism (Billy Abraham), liberation theology (José Míguez Bonino), theology of creation (Norman Young), and African theology (Canaan Banana).[10]

As the list suggests, almost every Methodist theologian has found specific possibilities for concretely discussing the meaning of God in human life. Theological exploration, even where it shares a common base, is remarkably diverse.

Because of this diversity, United Methodist theology is often thought to be undirected and without central emphases. But the unity of United Methodist theology is found in its beginnings, and in its ongoing efforts to relate this inheritance to present mission tasks.

In order to investigate the originating base of United Methodist theology, we shall follow the disciplinary statement and explore the Wesleyan quadrilateral that finds the foundations of theology in Scripture, tradition, experience, and reason. The meaning of the quadrilateral is the focus of the next chapter.

CHAPTER VII

The United Methodist Quadrilateral: Scripture and Tradition

*O*ne of the most characteristic features of United Methodist theology is the so-called Wesleyan Quadrilateral (pp. 80-86). The quadrilateral (which is a four-part frame of reference or four points of reference that shape theological study) is widely affirmed and utilized among teachers and preachers in United Methodism because it holds in relation Scripture, tradition, experience, and reason.

The quadrilateral was presented in a formal manner in the 1972 theological statement prepared for *The Discipline.* Although not explicitly found in John Wesley, the four criteria are true to Wesley's intention and style of theological work. Albert Outler has made a lasting contribution by elaborating these basic criteria.[11]

Acceptance of the quadrilateral within United Methodism was immediate because the guidelines expressed the Church's self-understanding. The quadrilateral focuses on Jesus Christ and serves the presentation of Jesus Christ. Consequently, appeal to and use of the quadrilateral has become characteristic of this theological tradition. If anything can be said to identify the distinctiveness of United Methodist theological method, it is the conscious employment of the quadrilateral.

SETTING THE FRAMEWORK

Some people assume that, once these guidelines are named, the resources and boundaries for theological work are clear. For instance, when we say Scripture or experience we have clear and consistent meanings in mind. But there is no simple clarity.

To state the four guidelines does not fully define an adequate theological base. The four elements indicate significant places of beginning, but they also indicate much work to be done. For example, we speak of Scripture as a source, but what do we mean by the authority of Scripture? How is Scripture to be interpreted? What is the nature of revelation in Scripture?

We can also ask questions of the meaning of experience. Are we referring to every experience? To particular experiences? To the experience of a special group? The same sort of questions can also be asked of tradition and reason. This questioning points to the fact that each of these guidelines for theological reflection needs to be clarified so that agreement about their meaning has more firmness.

In this chapter and in the following, we are not attempting to reach a single or solid definition for each guideline; that is the ongoing work of theology. Rather, we are attempting to portray how United Methodists do theology. Therefore, we are describing the framework of that activity. Once this framework is clear, then we should go on to clarify each of these guidelines.

Another issue of framework is clarifying the goal of theology in the United Methodist tradition. Theology is not an end in itself, rather it has practical implications for the transformation of life. Theology ought to serve the development of Christian character, the formation of Christian community, and the mission of the church in the world.

Theology, in this tradition, is subordinate to mission. Interpretation of faith is to help the gospel to be understood more truly, to be proclaimed more faithfully, and to be lived more authentically.

Consequently, as we discuss the guidelines for theology—whether Scripture, tradition, experience, or reason—we are not primarily concerned with speculative, intellectual issues. Rather, we discuss each of these themes to see how they serve the larger transformative tasks of the Christian gospel.

With an awareness of the need to begin a search for clarity and of the need for theology to serve the church's mission, we turn to each of the guidelines. In this chapter we shall discuss Scripture and tradition, and in the next, experience and reason.

SCRIPTURE

Christian Scripture is the primary source and criterion for doctrine and the most basic guide for theological exploration. The section on Scripture in the disciplinary statement is carefully crafted and merits detailed study (pp. 81-83).

To set the importance of Scripture, we shall begin by reflecting on the authority of Scripture. Because Methodist traditions have always stressed God's sovereignty over Scripture and the necessity of inspiration of the Holy Spirit in the writing and interpretations of Scripture, Methodist emphasis has been not on the words of the Bible, but on God's use of those words. How, then, are we to understand Scripture's authority in the light of God's sovereignty?

Authority is that which possesses the power to shape the lives of individuals and communities. Moreover, authority is that which is acknowledged as possessing the right and worth to shape life.

There are three emphases in this statement. First, authority is an expression of power. Authority has the ability to order or structure human existence. But, second, authority is not pure power. Authority does not impose itself as an external, overwhelming force or as an insensitively domineering authority. Rather, authority presents itself so as to invite acknowledgement, acceptance, and responsive obedience. Third, authority is the primary factor in the shaping or molding of human life. To be a person or to be a community is to have an organizing authority or center.

With this definition, it is possible to see that any number of authorities might be organizing principles of human existence. Consequently, the authority acknowledged shapes a person or community.

The claims of rival authorities set the tension between the true God and false gods. Life sculpted around a false god is always deformed. Life ordered around the true God is shaped in the image of God as the body of Christ.

The Bible is an intermediate authority. It communicates the living God through the power of the Holy Spirit, so as to bring new life through communion with Jesus Christ. Scripture is not the final authority, but our Bible is a necessary and indispensable medium through which God as primary authority is presented, invites acknowledgment, and functions to integrate life around this divine center.

Jesus Christ is the authority of Christian life, and the formative power of Christ is made known through the witness of the Bible as this is made a vital power by the Holy Spirit.

Scripture, by the inspiration of the Holy Spirit, becomes the medium by which God presents Christ to us and evokes our responsive worship. Scripture functions to shape our life in Christ. In this sense, the Bible is authoritative.

The Wesleyan tradition, especially, has remained sensitive to the person, role, and enlivening activity of the Holy Spirit. This awareness has not always been sharp or unalloyed; and, indeed, at times it has not been given enough attention. Nevertheless, among Methodists in the late nineteenth and early twentieth centuries, central acknowledgment of the Holy Spirit kept alive the authority of Scripture. Emphasizing the guidance of the Holy Spirit prevented an exclusive attention to the written texts of the Bible. This position prevented the words in the Bible from being understood as authoritative in themselves; the latter position is often referred to as plenary inspiration or biblical inerrancy. Rather, stress on the inspiration of the Holy Spirit emphasizes the freedom of God to speak through the biblical words.

The interpreter of the biblical word has a role that must be sensitively employed. The interpreter of the word stands immediately and thoroughly indebted to the guidance of the Holy Spirit. Through study and prayer, he or she must be sensitive to the Holy Spirit's inspiring of the words of Scripture. The Holy Spirit guides interpretation in the community of faithful believers. The Bible possesses a derived authority from the Holy Spirit as it mediates Jesus Christ and effects the formation of life in Christ. Authority shapes life; Jesus Christ, as we know of him through Scripture, shapes Christian life. This occurs as the Holy Spirit operates as a pervasive presence for writers, interpreters, and hearers of the word.

The prayer for illumination that is offered just before the reading of the Scripture lessons in many United Methodist churches states a correct theological understanding.

> Lord, open our hearts and minds
> by the power of your Holy Spirit,
> that, as the Scriptures are read
> and your Word proclaimed, we may
> hear with joy what you have to say
> to us.

Scriptural authority functions to constitute and empower communal life. So it shapes liturgy and preaching, theological reflection and church education, and the organization and mission of the church.

Further, Scripture is authoritative as it encounters us within our particular social setting and leads us in our struggle to enact life as God's people in our historical setting. The authority of the Bible takes on its significance as we, through the agency of the Holy Spirit, are drawn into its orbit and as our situation, through the agency of the Holy Spirit, shapes our reception of the Bible's meaning.

In Methodist traditions, Scripture is primary. All other sources and guidelines—even tradition, experience, and reason—are secondary. All of the sources and criteria are important, and all are to be used. But that which is first and most basic is Scripture.

TRADITION

Tradition shapes every community and every interpreter. Tradition conveys language and culture, worship forms, and understanding of ethical responsibility. Yet, the rich complexity of human life means that we live at the intersection of more than one tradition.

For instance, I am an inheritor of Western culture, the English language, Enlightenment (or particular cultural) sensibilities, USA national values, a capitalistic economy, and Protestant and United Methodist Christian formation. (Every person would have to describe the ingredients of her own history.) However, even with this complexity some traditions are more basic, more formative than others. Hence we often use our basic tradition, such as Christian faith, to assess critically the values of our other influencing traditions.

We cannot be free from tradition. There is no place for human beings to stand above tradition, though some traditions are more self-critical and freeing than others. We are, necessarily and inescapably, tradition formed. We understand ourselves through tradition; our past is our past because we have come through a specific history, our present is given to us by these shaping influences, our future is set by the hopes of our primary tradition. (Read again the foreword of this book.)

The influence of traditions on us is of various strength. For each person there is priority among traditions; but there is no purity of a tradition. Consequently, constant struggle is required to be clear about our basic tradition. For persons whose lives are authoritatively shaped by Jesus Christ, the most influential tradition should be the Christian community of their concrete church.

It is within this United Methodist Church framework that the theological statement in *The Discipline* must be set (pp. 83-84). The statement attempts to make clear the primacy of the Christian tradition that is mediated through our particular United Methodist history.[12]

We are open to what other traditions have to say to us, yet our particular church tradition identifies us and provides us, at least in part, with criteria by which we affirm, modify, or reject the values in other traditions.

Yet, Christian tradition, as United Methodists perceive it, is one that reflects back on its originator, Jesus Christ, as Scripture and earlier tradition bears witness to him. This is the originating point out of which our tradition is shaped. The Bible is the core of this written tradition.

We are also debtors to other persons too numerous to name. But we read, revere, and learn from such persons as Augustine, Bernard, Aquinas, Luther, and Calvin. We read and acknowledge the Nicean and Chalcedonian Creeds, and practical and sacramental developments. We come from the Church of England and the Protestant Reformation.

We are special debtors to John and Charles and Susanna Wesley, Francis Asbury, name-forgotten Circuit Riders, Jacob Albright and William Philip Otterbein, Episcopal Methodism, Methodist Protestants, Evangelical United Brethren, and theological leaders such as Nathan Bangs, Georgia Harkness, Albert C. Knudson, and Edwin Lewis. To mention only these few makes us aware of the richness and influence of our most direct United Methodist tradition.

We must also remember the forms of our worship, church school nurture, our hymnody, our shared mission, and our conference affiliations. Our tradition is made up of all of the influences that have shaped our spiritual existence as we have been nurtured in Christian faith through United Methodism.

When we undertake theological tasks we ask not only, what guidance on this subject do we derive from Scripture? But also, what has the tradition had to say about this subject? Biblical and historical study are basic to serious United Methodist theological activity.

CHAPTER VIII

The United Methodist Quadrilateral: Experience and Reason

*E*lements of the quadrilateral that identify the guidelines for United Methodist theology include experience and reason in addition to Scripture and tradition. These elements focus on who the triune God is and what the Christian gospel means.

Once again, we need to restate the fact that each of these elements of theology is subject to multiple interpretations and this is especially true in regard to experience. In our discussion, we want to indicate the importance of these guidelines in setting the frame of reference for United Methodist theology.

With emphasis on experience and reason, the resources are specified in even more personal and immediate terms. We must be careful not to separate too sharply between objective and subjective, external and internal dimensions of human experience, for the dual emphases are finally inseparable.

The written message of Scripture as it is received through the internal witness of the Holy Spirit combines both internal and external dimensions. Tradition possesses vitality both as given and received and these dimensions are bound together. Religious experience is not solely internal. Our experiences of God are shaped by God's encounter with us as well as our response to that encounter. There are other external influences—such as race, gender, culture, and social status—that also shape our reception even as we reshape their meaning. Even reason is not a private, individual activity, but represents our making use of traditions of received language, logic, argument, evidence, and value. We live in relation to external factors, even as we utilize these influences in our own way.

With experience and reason we reach into arenas that stress the emotions, affections, or rational dimensions of human life. Once again, United Methodist theology attempts a Christian interpretation that encompasses the total person in the whole range of personhood. In attempting to achieve such wholeness, we shall see how these two factors serve as sources for theology.

EXPERIENCE

Notice must be taken of the variety of interpretations of this theme. But precisely because of this variety and because of the importance of this theme, ongoing clarification is a major theological task.

One of the distinctive emphases in Wesleyan theology is its stress on personal experience; that is, a personal acceptance of the meaning of the

Christian gospel. Put more plainly: Methodist theology emphasizes a personal, lively, engaging relationship with Jesus Christ.

To be Christian is to live with God. It is to live in relationship with Jesus Christ in such a way that he is our Lord, our guide, the center of our affections, the inspirer of our service, the object of our worship, and the friend who sustains us.

The Holy Spirit is God present. To experience God's presence is to be engaged by the presence of the Holy Spirit. Hence, Christian experience is to live in relationship to God as redeemer, God as creator, and God as ever-present reality—all of which is mediated by the Holy Spirit.

As used in this theological context, experience is—first of all and most of all—experience of relationship through the Holy Spirit with Jesus Christ. All other experience is secondary and subordinate. Every other arena of experience, however significant, whether shaped by race or gender or culture or society, is looked at and valued from the perspective of relationship with Jesus Christ.

These other shapers of experience may and do contribute to our interpretation of Christian faith. All of us need to hear what Christian faith means to people, especially those who are unlike us. But the reality that holds all Christians together is Jesus Christ who transcends us all, but who establishes the primary relationship of Christian existence.

Our experience situates us in relation to God who speaks to us through Scripture; it places us within our tradition; and it influences the way we employ reason.

Obviously, we can recognize different levels of experience. Each of us experiences—receives, evaluates, reacts to—reality in terms of our place in the world: our race, with its special history and present characterizations; our gender, with its status and role; our culture, with its nurture of sensibilities and sympathies; and our society with its power and restraint.

Everyone experiences the world through such filters. Yet, even among this variety of influences, we can distinguish levels of importance. For some, race will be dominant, for others gender, for others culture or social conditions, and for others some combination of these factors.

What makes Christian experience *Christian* is that, in the last analysis, all other shaping factors of experience are brought under the transforming relationship with Jesus Christ. This primary relationship affects the interpretation of every other condition or experience of life. This relationship is the most fundamental, the most influential, the deepest experience of all.

Yet, the relationship with Jesus Christ is realized only through these other dimensions of our existence. Relationship with Jesus Christ is not abstract, but historical; it does not occur apart from our social location, but engages us how and where we live. Jesus Christ relates to us as we are, as we actually are. Jesus Christ both judges and fulfills who we actually are.

To be engaged in theological exploration as United Methodists is to take seriously the historical realm. It is to examine the interplay of sets of experience. It is to assess the friction among aspects of experience, to see how they do and ought to relate to one another. It is to attempt to understand the relevance of the Christian gospel for the actual conditions of human existence.

In theological discussion, we must ask certain questions. How much does or should race, whatever our race, shape our theology? How much should our being male or female determine our theology? How much should culture or nationality, economic conditions or educational background shape our efforts to interpret God, our world, and ourselves?

Every perspective is partial, yet every perspective can discern an aspect of the more comprehensive truth. How do the various perspectives give character to our interpretation of the Christian gospel?

No area of theological activity at the present time is more complex, difficult, divisive, or necessary than that of experience. Many questions press for attention. What sorts of experiences are to be taken seriously? How do we set priorities among experiences? How does the experience of Jesus Christ shape these other experiences? How do other experiences shape our experience of Jesus Christ? Such questions make theology vital.

To avoid these questions is to allow Christian faith to become irrelevant and lacking in concrete meaning. On the other hand, to run with every current of changing sensibility is to wash out the distinctive character of Christian faith.

There are no simple formulas for maintaining the appropriate tension among our experiences. But a part of the ongoing theological struggle is to learn ways of negotiating the claims and counterclaims of experience in the light of the other parts of the quadrilateral.

REASON

John Wesley had great confidence in common sense. He was, at times, overly trusting in human capacity to think through matters and to come to a clear conclusion. With confidence in observation and in the ability to draw reasonable conclusions, Wesley attempted to make his presentation of the Christian faith rationally convincing—that is, he wrote in a clear, well-organized style.

Wesley's followers have prized clear and persuasive reasoning and have believed such capacity for reasoning is a distinctive human capability. In North America, this confidence has been present from the beginning, starting with Nathan Bangs, the first American Wesleyan theologian. Bangs was interested in coming into discussion with dominant philosophical schools of thought; and this interest has continued through the Methodist theological tradition.

In Western culture, especially for the last two centuries, there has been a dominant conviction that rational thought is an independent, free-standing means of assessing the world. Rationality has been taken to be purely objective, that is to say, a detached, neutral way of viewing the world. All we want is the facts. Every clue is to be unemotionally considered. To allow value or emotion to intrude would distort the matter. Such an attitude has been taken to be the truly scientific way of thinking.

But this understanding is now often questioned. We have come to see that theory shapes facts even more than facts develop into theory; value and fact are inseparable; scientific knowledge begins with a world view, as well as passion and personal commitment. To separate the mind and the emotions distorts both our thinking and our feeling. Personal experience includes our thoughts, our feelings, and our actions. One or another factor may be stressed, but no one factor can be emphasized to the exclusion of the others.

Reason is a tool for theology. But it must be modest in its claims, aware of its relation to the other sources, and careful to take into account its own formation by tradition and community. Reason is a guide for theology in that theology must pass through the winnowing of thoughtful consideration.

To ask if a theological expression is reasonable is not to compare theological statements to some independent nontheological standard of what is to be believed. Rather, it is to ask are the ideas consistent with one another? Is what is said about humans as sinners consistent with what is said about Jesus Christ as savior? Is the theological expression faithful to the Christian gospel of grace? Have the interplay of Scripture, tradition, experience, and reason been taken adequately into account?

The Holy Spirit plays an important role in our reasoning. To say, "Let's be reasonable," is not a conclusion, as though reasoning is a matter of simple human effort. To be reasonable is to attempt to think with the guidance of the Holy Spirit. Our thought may be inspired by the Holy Spirit, who helps us by instruction, guidance, correction, and fresh insight.

Ability to reason competently needs nurture, correction, and enhancement. Reason as found in sinful people operates out of a different value system geared toward different goals and is often judged by different standards than the reasoning of a person who attempts to love and serve God.

In chapter 3, we stressed that true alignment with God is the precondition for understanding the truth of God and the truth of the human condition. This is what has sometimes been called right reason. The content of Christian knowledge depends on a relationship with God.

People outside of Christian faith can challenge us to take specific issues into account. They can challenge our logic, they can even challenge us to see what we should see. But the actual content of faith, what should be said about God and the world, is known in a relationship with God, and not primarily in relation to the challenges of the world.

Reason is not, therefore, an independent and neutral sovereign that establishes truth. Reason serves the truth—Jesus Christ. Christian or theological reason is faith seeking understanding, which means that faith and reason are tightly connected. Reason needs faith for its motivation and ultimate direction; faith needs reason for its elaboration.

Reason is one guideline, along with the others, for theological interpretation. In relation to Scripture, tradition, and experience, reason contributes to the understanding of God.

In the Wesleyan tradition, reason is understood primarily as practical reason, reason that serves the transformation of life. Reason is not so much to be valued because it can control the world, but because it produces wisdom about how to live in Christian community and as Christians in our social setting. Rationality serves the ordering of life as worship and service of God.

THE COMPLETE QUADRILATERAL

We have made a quick survey of the four elements in the quadrilateral: Scripture, tradition, experience, and reason. We have said that for United Methodists all four may function as guidelines for theology. All four serve mutually to check and to enrich each other.

All of the quadrilateral emphases point to Jesus Christ. Jesus Christ is the center around which all of these elements come together. None of the elements is freestanding; they support one another in making clear who Jesus Christ is and what the gospel means. All of the guidelines are pointing in one direction: That we may know Jesus Christ.

However, one of the four elements has priority. In company with Protestant traditions, the basic emphasis is on Scripture. Scripture is the primary source because it is the most historically direct witness to Jesus Christ. Scripture is the fountainhead of theological reflection. Hence, the Bible is the first among equals in the United Methodist quadrilateral.

Scripture does not stand alone in some pure state. The Bible is historically produced and interpreted. Consequently, Christians are radically dependent on the inspiration of the Holy Spirit in the gift of Scripture and in the interpretation of Scripture. Tradition, experience, and reason are used by the Holy Spirit in the interpretation of Scripture and thus, though primary, the authority of Scripture cannot exist without the other three.

Each of these subordinate guidelines has multiple possible characterizations and various interpretations. As with Scripture, each of these elements is open to misuse. Not only may the "Devil make use of Scripture for his own purposes," but also tradition, experience, and reason may be used to distort or misinterpret the Christian message.

At this juncture it becomes clear why a faithful community is of basic importance in theological activity. A community of faithful people provides the necessary setting for theology; they join together in prayer, invoke the guidance of the Holy Spirit, discuss with integrity, assess tradition, probe Christian experience (past and present), and make rational interpretations of faith. Christian community nurtures, directs, shares, corrects, and emboldens theological work.

Communities themselves may become captured by false interpretation, by parochial emphasis, or by narrow vision. Thus tradition is important to guard against such misinterpretation, as each community is set within the larger, and more inclusive, Christian movement. Tradition gives a vote, but not a veto, to the past. It also points to the future and to those who are still to join the great "cloud of witnesses." (Heb. 12:1)

Theological work is continual, it must go on; God's full truth requires continual reformulation, correction, and enrichment. The quadrilateral sets points of reference that provide authentic guidance for United Methodists in this effort of exploration.

We conclude this discussion of the quadrilateral by repeating a caution in regard to what may appear to be a deceptive simplicity about these four guidelines. Each one may appear to be clear and constant in its meaning. But, in fact, each element requires careful definition and constant attention.

United Methodists are in agreement that these four points of reference are important and that all four need to be used. The discussion of these guidelines and their relationships characterizes theology in our church.

CHAPTER IX

Catching Up . . . Going Ahead

Far from wishing you to be ignorant of any of our doctrines, or any part of our discipline, we desire you to read, mark, learn, and inwardly digest the whole. We know you are not in general able to purchase many books: but you ought, next to the word of God, to procure the Articles and Canons of the Church to which you belong.[13]

We have taken a rather long journey through United Methodist ways of understanding Christian faith and some of the basic content of that faith. As a reminder, we can mention some of the emphases we have made through this journey. Such a summary may help draw together the various themes we have discussed.

But we also need to go beyond a simple drawing together of previously discussed issues, much as a spectator might recall the plays in a football game. We need to hear again the invitation to become participants in understanding our faith. A part of what it means to be in The United Methodist Church is to take the responsibility of understanding our faith for ourselves and of presenting our Christian faith to others.

DRAWING EMPHASES TOGETHER

We begin by recalling, in summary form, what we have studied along the way. We are shaped by our tradition. No one begins the Christian life without a history. These histories vary greatly, but United Methodists share a common point of beginning in the Wesleyan revival movement in eighteenth-century England. From this source, there have developed forms of worship, styles of preaching and singing, special emphases on serving social principles, organizational patterns, disciplines of discipleship, particular mission concerns, and distinctive interpretations of our faith.

Traditions are the movement of corporate bodies over time. Traditions embody the developing, changing, supportive life of a community. United Methodism has a particular history as a community of believers, believers who share common—but not narrow and restrictive—forms of responding to God. We have been nurtured by this tradition that forms our background and challenges us to maturity.

To possess a name is to have a tradition. But traditions are never static, they are fluid, and constantly in the process of being reformed. We have a name, United Methodist; we have a tradition, our Wesleyan history; and we have a future, our intention to be faithful to the will of God.

The United Methodist tradition has roots in the wide family of Christian believers. We recognize kinship with the largest possible extended family.

Our movement began with deep indebtedness to Christians who had gone before. And these rich gifts are happily acknowledged.

But the Wesleyan revival movement has been distinctive because of the way in which it has molded its inheritance and has given it forms.

The Wesleyan tradition is not primarily theological, for it has stressed mission and faithful discipleship. But the United Methodist tradition is also theological, for its mission, its witness, and the forms of its discipleship are based on its understanding of God, who has come to us as creator, in Jesus Christ, and as Holy Spirit.

United Methodism has a distinctive theological character: Theology serves the transformation of life. This is to say, theology is not an end in itself. In this regard, United Methodist theology is unlike theology in many other Christian traditions. In the Wesleyan tradition, theology is not primarily an intellectual task that can be satisfied by rational explanations. In sharp difference, the chief goal of theology in our tradition is to make preaching more adequate, to make discipleship more faithful, and to make our witness a true representation of God's nature and will.

John Wesley had several things to say about theology and its importance. In "The Character of a Methodist," he states, "The distinguishing marks of a Methodist are not his opinions of any sort. His assenting to this or that scheme of religion, his embracing any particular set of notions."[14] He goes on, in a letter, to lift up the importance of living faith. "But what is faith? Not an opinion, no more than it is a form of words; not any number of opinions put together, be they ever so true."[15]

Justifying faith implies, not only a divine *elenchos* [i.e. persuasion], that "God was in Christ reconciling the world unto himself," but a sure confidence that Christ died for *my* sins, that he loved *me*, and gave himself for *me*. And the moment a penitent sinner believes this, God pardons and absolves him.[16]

The point of Wesley's comments is that theology may be no more than a play with words, a clash of opinions, or a dead orthodoxy. In contrast, Wesley believed that theology should serve to enhance faith, that is, a living relationship with God. Only as theology helps to proclaim Christian faith and assists Christian maturity does it possess importance. This is what Wesley means by *Practical Divinity* (Theology)—namely, thinking about God should enable authentic living with God. This understanding has characterized theology in the Methodist traditions: Theology is important as it aids the transformation of life.

Theology, as developed in the traditions that merged into United Methodism, possesses consistent family traits. Salvation is offered to all people; belief is related to action. The love of God is related to the service of God. Thought is inseparably bound to love and action. The most pervasive theme is grace.

We have seen, in our main discussion, that our tradition shares many theological themes with other Christian bodies. In our Articles of Religion and in the Evangelical United Brethren Creed, we affirm: God as triune, the Father as creator, the mystery of salvation in Jesus Christ, the living presence of the Holy Spirit, the oneness of the Church of Jesus Christ, the reign of God, and the authority of Scripture. All of these we hold in common with

most other Christians. And we proudly count ourselves among their ranks.

We, as United Methodists, have also developed a
series of theological emphases that are especially
our own. Other Christians certainly share many of
these convictions. But the concentration on these
themes and the development of them in our interpretation of the Christian life means that they
define in clear ways who we are.

It might be more accurate to say that these
themes developed our tradition more than our tradition developed these themes. These understandings are the foundation on which United Methodist
worship, spirituality, mission, service, and interpretation have been built.

Many summaries of the main themes of United
Methodist theology have been offered. There is consistency in emphases, even if there is a difference in
order or arrangement. Robert E. Cushman, for
instance, has provided one short statement of these
primary themes.

The four living stones, foundational for the structure of
early Methodism, have been scanned. They are:
Christian perfection as the goal of human life, justification by faith as the way to it, radical sinfulness as the
barrier to be overcome, and faith that works by love as
the normal fruit of the renovated life. What we have seen
is that, always clear as he was about the nature of the
Christian life, Wesley, until 1738, did not understand the
way of attainment. In 1733 he was requiring "circumci-
sion of the heart" and unqualified love to God and man.
But he did not yet acknowledge these as the fruits of
faith, that faith itself is a gift of grace, and that the gift-
ing carries with it a renewal of the image of God in man,
that is, in St. Paul's language, a "new creation."[17]

99

The particular beliefs that have characterized United Methodism are all rooted in grace, for grace has been our central theme. Yet, we have stressed specific dimensions of grace.

We begin with prevenient grace—God's going before us, God taking the initiative in every relationship. We know, at the deepest level of our being, we love God because God first loved us.

The human need of grace is built upon the sharp awareness of the sinful condition of human beings. A radical separation from God characterizes human existence. We who were created by God for relationship with God have rejected that relationship. We attempt to live without God and, thereby, distort human life. As sinners, we are in need of reconciliation with God.

Justification is God's free love, which reclaims us for covenant relationship. God's forgiveness restores the broken relationship. Regeneration is the result of justification and is God's work in us. Assurance is confidence that God's love never fails. In the actions of justification, regeneration, and assurance we acknowledge that our new life in Christ is given and sustained by God. It is all of grace.

Sanctification and perfection point to the goal of Christian maturity. Once again, the theme is grace. We are not spiritually self-made; Christian goodness is not a human achievement. God works in us and with us to lead us to full growth in Christian life. The goal of mature—indeed perfect—love of God is a distinctive emphasis in our tradition.

The dynamic relation between faith and good works is held tight. One cannot say that one loves God but does not love one's neighbor (I John 4:9).

Works without faith have inadequate motive or sustaining power. Faith without works is hollow and is not an expression of responsible discipleship.

United Methodism is a church that is defined primarily by its mission. This church is formed by its mission to share the gospel of grace in gracious ways. The two are inseparable: The church is the body of Christ given for the world; worship and service are two parts of a single reality.

Can an ideal Methodist be profiled? In a general way perhaps, for the character of a Methodist is that of a person who lives in covenant with the triune God, who lives as a part of the body of Christ, and who lives for the kingdom of God. Further, a person formed by the United Methodist tradition rejoices in God's prevenient grace and in God's justifying and sanctifying grace. That person's faith is lived out in good works and his or her purpose in life is found through sharing in the mission of the church.

Such a character sketch also describes the Methodist theologian. A theologian in this tradition shares in all of these means of life-formation, and her or his theological effort is directed to understanding and presenting these basic themes. In part this is done by making our doctrines clear; in part this is done through fresh theological exploration. In all, this is done by holding our thought, our love, and our service together.

Traditions are constantly extending in new directions. The theological task of United Methodism is to help guide these new extensions by bringing our received doctrine and theology into contemporary interpretations through constructive and critical effort, by being aware of individual and communal aspects of faith and life, by taking our historical context with utter seriousness, and by keeping the end of the theological activity focused on the practical life.

To say all of this quickly is to attempt to say too much. But perhaps it makes clear that, with John Wesley, we want to live obediently to the great commandments: To love God with our whole heart, mind, and strength; and to love our neighbors as ourselves.

A RENEWED INVITATION

The final major emphasis in our study is to renew the invitation issued in the first chapter. Every United Methodist is invited to the daunting but joyful task of becoming involved in interpreting and presenting our Christian faith.

EPILOGUE

The Character of a
Methodist Theologian

John Wesley wrote a tract titled "The Character of a Methodist."[18] The pamphlet has been republished many times and has won wide approval as a statement of Methodist spirit. In a playfully serious vein, I want freely to edit and add to this tract so as to indicate the character of a United Methodist theologian. To remain somewhat aligned with Wesley's usage, I shall simply use the word Methodist.

1. The distinguishing marks of a Methodist theologian are not opinions of any sort. Assenting to this or that scheme of religion, embracing any particular set of notions, espousing the judgment of one person or of another, are all quite wide of the point. We believe, indeed, that all Scripture is given by the inspiration of God; we believe the written word of God to be the only and sufficient rule both of Christian faith and practice; and we believe Christ to be the eternal, supreme God. But as to all opinions that do not strike at the root of Christianity, we think and let think.

2. We do not place our religion, or any part of it, in being attached to any peculiar mode of speaking,

any quaint or uncommon set of expressions. The most obvious, easy, and common words, wherein our meaning can be conveyed, we prefer before others, both on ordinary occasions, and when we speak of the things of God. So it is as gross an error to place the marks of a Methodist theologian in his or her words, as in opinions of any sort.

3. Nor do we desire to be distinguished by actions, customs, or usages, of an indifferent nature. Our religion does not lie in doing what God has not enjoined, or abstaining from what God hath not forbidden. Therefore, neither will any one, who knows whereof they affirm, fix the mark of a Methodist theologian here.

4. Nor, lastly, is a Methodist theologian distinguished by laying the whole stress of religion on any single part of it. If you say, Yes, he or she is: For they think we are saved by faith alone; I answer, You do not understand the terms. By salvation we mean holiness of heart and life. And this we affirm to spring from true faith alone. We do not place the whole of religion (as many do, God knoweth) either in doing no harm, or in doing good, or in using the ordinances of God. No, not in all of them together; wherein we know by experience a person may labor many years, and at the end have no religion at all, no more than she or he had at the beginning.

5. What then is the mark? Who is a Methodist theologian according to your own account? I answer: A Methodist theologian is one who has the love of God shed abroad in his or her heart by the Holy Ghost given unto them; one who loves God with all her heart, with all his soul, and with all his or her mind and strength. God is the joy of such a heart, and the desire of such a soul.

A Methodist theologian is one who hath been set true in relation to God and who seeks truthful understanding and expression of who God is. There is wholeness of thought and life. With humble courage, the gospel is served through critical and constructive interpretations of our Christian faith.

6. A Methodist theologian is therefore happy in God, yea, always happy, as having a well of water springing up into everlasting life. For one that believeth, hath the witness: being now the child of God by faith. And the Spirit itself beareth witness with our spirit, that we are children of God. Our joy is full, and our bones cry out, Blessed be the God and Father of our Lord Jesus Christ, who, according to his abundant mercy, hath begotten me again to a living hope—of an inheritance incorruptible, undefiled, and that fadeth not away, reserved in heaven for me!

Incorporated into Christ, the Methodist theologian lives within Christian community and speaks about belief from within this community. Shaped by the Wesleyan tradition, such a person contributes to the preservation and new growth of this tradition.

7. The theologian has this hope and in everything gives thanks. Everywhere and in all things we are instructed to both be full and to be hungry, both to abound and suffer need. The theologian is therefore careful (anxious or uneasy) for nothing: as having cast care on God that cares for him or her.

The Methodist theologian stresses the theme of grace: prevenient grace, justifying grace, sanctifying grace. Grace is the most basic and most thorough affirmation of God.

8. For indeed, the Methodist theologian prays without ceasing. At all times the language of the heart is this: Thou brightness of the eternal glory, unto thee is my heart, though without a voice, and my silence speaketh unto thee. In retirement or company, in leisure, business, or conversation, the theologian's heart is ever with the Lord.

The Methodist theologian is concerned with practical matters, with the transformative power of the Christian gospel. Therefore, his or her theological work is to serve the establishing and growth of new being in Jesus Christ.

9. The Methodist theologian loves the neighbor, indeed loves every one, including one's enemies; yea, and the enemies of God—the evil and the unthankful.

The incarnate character of Christian love is reinforced by careful theological consideration of contemporary issues, with special regard to both personal and communal aspects of faith and life, and by taking the concrete historical setting as the arena of God's activity.

10. The Methodist theologian is pure in heart. The love of God has purified the heart from all revengeful passions, from envy, malice, and wrath, from every unkind temper or malign affection. It has been cleansed from pride and haughtiness of spirit, whereof alone comes contention. And one has now put on bowels of mercy, kindness, humbleness of mind, meekness, longsuffering. And, indeed, all possible ground for contention is utterly cut off. For all desire is unto God, and to the remembrance of God's name.

Piety and faithfulness characterize the Methodist theologian's style of life. Responsible discipleship is expressed in faith working through love, in missional service, in efforts to understand God, and in the worship of God.

11. The Methodist theologian's one intention at all times and in all things is not to please himself or herself, but God who is loved. When the eye is single, the whole body is full of light. God then reigns alone. Every thought that arises points to God, and is in obedience to the law of Christ.

Ecumenical in spirit, open to reform, engaged in witness, the theologian both rejoices in our rich Christian heritage and develops an interpretation nurtured by the United Methodist tradition. All of this is in order to serve God more completely and the neighbor more faithfully.

12. A tree is known by its fruits. So the Methodist theologian loves God and keeps God's commandments. Whatever God has forbidden is avoided; whatever God hath enjoined is done.

Scripture, tradition, experience, and reason are guidelines honored and kept in tight relation to one another. Rightly dividing the word of truth, the Methodist theologian maintains breadth and intensity in order to give range and focus to the task of exploring fresh theological meaning.

13. All the commandments of God are kept and that with all might. Obedience is in proportion to love, the source from whence it flows. And therefore, loving God with all one's heart, we serve God with all our strength. We continually present soul and body as a living sacrifice, holy, acceptable to God. All the talents received are constantly employed according to God's will; every power and faculty of soul, every member of body is yielded as an instrument of righteousness unto God.

The Methodist theologian is especially sensitive to the arenas of life that require transformation—personal and social. Those who have been formed by sin are presented with the reforming power of the gospel. Social structures that are malformed by injustice are challenged by the power of the righteousness of God.

14. By consequence, whatsoever the Methodist theologian does, it is all to the glory of God. In all employments of every kind, she or he not only aims at this (which is implied in having a single eye) but actually attains it. Business and refreshment as well as prayers all serve this great end. The one invariable rule is this: Whatever ye do, in word or deed, do it all in the name of the Lord Jesus, giving thanks to God and the Father by him.

The intellectual love of God characterizes the theological task and the theologian's singular work. The achievements of intellectual work are offerings to God.

15. Nor do the customs of the world at all hinder his or her running the race that is set before them. They cannot utter an unkind word of any one; for love keeps the door of the lips. No idle words, no corrupt communication ever comes out of their mouth. But whatsoever things are pure, whatsoever things are lovely, whatsoever things are of good report, the theologian speaks.

With words rightly chosen, the theologian attempts to speak the truth in love, knowing that wisdom comes from the Lord. For the fear of the Lord is the beginning of wisdom and in Jesus Christ we know the truth and the truth shall set us free.

16. Lastly, the Methodist theologian does good unto all people, unto neighbors and strangers,

friends, and enemies. And that in every possible kind not only to their bodies by feeding the hungry, clothing the naked, visiting those that are sick or in prison, but much more to do good to their souls, to awaken those that sleep in death, to bring those who are awakened to the atoning blood, that being justified by faith, they may have peace with God, and to provoke those who have peace with God to abound more in love and in good works.

Dealing with concrete historical situations, the Methodist theologian deals with actual human conditions. The gospel, rightly understood, places those who have responded to its call in immediate relation to the world. Both personal and corporate, both individual and structural dimensions of experience are engaged and challenged to redemption.

17. These are the principles and practices of our societies; these are the marks of a true Methodist theologian. If any one say, "Why, these are only the common fundamental principles of Christianity!" This is the truth; I know they are no other; and I would to God both thou and all people knew, that I, and all who follow my judgment, do vehemently refuse to be distinguished from others by any but the common principles of Christianity—the plain, old Christianity I teach, renouncing and detesting all other marks of distinction.

The Methodist theologian rejoices both in the common gifts from the Christian traditions and in the special gifts from the United Methodist tradition. Affirming our doctrines, the theologian also accepts the task of courageously proclaiming the gospel to the world.

18. By these marks, by these fruits of a living faith, do we labor to distinguish ourselves from the

unbelieving world, from all those whose minds or lives are not according to the gospel of Christ. But from real Christians, or whatsoever denomination they be, we earnestly desire not to be distinguished at all, not from any who sincerely follow after what they know they have not yet attained. No: "Whosoever does the will of God is my brother and sister and mother" (Mark 3:35). And I beseech you, brethren, by the mercies of God, that we be in no wise divided among ourselves. Is thy heart right, as my heart is with thine? I ask no farther question. If it be, give me thy hand. For opinions, or terms, let us not destroy the work of God. Dost thou love and serve God? It is enough. I give thee the right hand of fellowship.

NOTES

1. *The Book of Discipline of The United Methodist Church*
   (Nashville: The United Methodist Publishing House,
   1988), p. 79; hereafter parenthetical page numbers in
   the text will refer to this volume.
2. Dante Alighieri, *The Divine Comedy, Paradiso,* Canto
   XXVII, lines 130-139.
3. Herbert Butterfield, *Christianity and History* (New
   York: Charles Scribner's Sons, 1950), p. 146.
4. This book is an effort to set in context, clarify, and
   comment on these paragraphs. Hence the primary
   source for the study of theological discussions in
   United Methodism is to be found in *The Discipline.*
5. For a more complete discussion of the authority of
   General Conference in the formulation of doctrine for
   the United Methodist Church, see my article, "The
   Teaching Office in United Methodism," *Quarterly
   Review,* Fall 1990, pp. 4-17.
6. For the most complete report on the processes, see the
   articles by Richard P. Heitzenrater, "In Search of
   Consensus," and Thomas A. Langford, "Conciliar
   Theology: A Report," both found in *Doctrine and
   Theology in the United Methodist Church* (Atlanta:
   Kingswood Books, 1990).
7. See *The Discipline* for references to Doctrinal
   Standards, pp. 53-77.
8. For an account of the disciplinary statement that has
   been prepared for church study groups, and directed

primarily to lay people, see Kenneth L. Carder, *Doctrinal Standards and Our Theological Task,* Leader's Guide (Nashville: Graded Press, 1989). An inexpensive pamphlet that contains only the theological section of *The Discipline* may also be purchased from the Graded Press and is a useful tool for group study.

9. See paragraphs 101-107 in *The Discipline,* pp. 112-14. For a more complete discussion of mission in the United Methodist Church, see Thomas A. Langford, "Grace upon Grace, God's Mission and Ours" (Nashville: Graded Press, 1990).

10. To refer to specific theologians in such a terse fashion is potentially distorting. I make these notations not to capture the contributions of these representative theologians, but to point to their significance. The hope is that mention of them will st imulate study of them.

11. See for further discussion, Outler's article, "The Wesleyan Quadrilateral," reprinted in Thomas A. Langford, ed., *Doctrine and Theology in The United Methodist Church* (Nashville: Kingswood Books, 1990). For further discussion of the framework issues, see, Thomas A. Langford, "The United Methodist Quadrilateral: A Theological Task," in Langford, ed., *Doctrine and Theology in The United Methodist Church.*

12. United Methodists have been especially interested in their history, almost in a unique way among North American Protestants. (On this, see Russell Richey's article in Thomas A. Langford, ed. *Doctrine and Theology in The United Methodist Church.*)

13. John Wesley, *Doctrines and Discipline* (1798), preface, p. IV.

14. *Works,* ed. Thomas Jackson, 3rd ed. (London: Wesley Methodist Book Room, 1872), VIII, 340.

15. Letter to the Reverend Dr. Conyers Middleton, *ibid.,* X, 72.

16. "A Farther Appeal," *The Works of John Wesley*, ed., Frank Baker (Oxford: Oxford University Press, 1975), XI, 116-17.
17. *Faith Seeking Understanding* (Durham: Duke University Press, 1981), p. 61.
18. *Works*, ed. Thomas Jackson, VIII, pp. 340-41.

INDEX